# NICOLAS MALEBRANCHE:

## Dialogue Between
## a Christian Philosopher
## and a Chinese Philosopher
## on the
## Existence and Nature of God

Translation and Introduction
by
Dominick A. Iorio

University Press
of America™

Copyright © 1980 by

**University Press of America, Inc.**
4710 Auth Place, S.E., Washington, D.C. 20023

ISBN: 0-8191-1027-2
Cloth Bound

ISBN: 0-8191-1028-0
Paper Bound

Library of Congress Catalog Card Number: 80-5045

To my wife, Stella

2119829

## ACKNOWLEDGMENTS

This brief volume would not have seen the light of day had it not been for the understanding and cooperation of Professor André Robinet and the Director of the Librairie Philosophique (Vrin), Monsieur Gérard Paulhac. Both these gentlemen deserve and are extended my sincere gratitude.

My gratitude is due also to Mrs. Mildred Scarpati and Miss Barbara Harris for their generous assistance in the preparation of this volume. I wish to acknowledge, in addition, the help and encouragement provided me by my colleague, Dr. Yash Nandan of the Department of Sociology at Rider College.

Finally, my thanks go to my colleagues in the Department of Philosophy at Rider College and to Dr. Elizabeth Salmon who fifteen years ago revealed to her students the originality and vigor of Malebranche's philosophy. Her seminars at Fordham University are fondly and gratefully recalled.

# CONTENTS

## PREFACE

Although Nicolas Malebranche has been called
the greatest metaphysician of France next to Rene
Descartes, he has until recently been one of the
most neglected major French thinkers. This neg-
lect has been apparent even in his own country,
despite the remarkable popularity he enjoyed in
his own day and the far-reaching influence he ex-
ercised on several of the central philosophic
figures of the seventeenth and eighteenth centuries. Among these may be included Wilhelm
Leibniz, George Berkeley and Pierre Bayle, as
well as numerous lesser luminaries of those centuries.

In America, unfortunately, Malebranche is still
practically unknown to and certainly not often
appreciated by the philosophically literate. No
more than three major studies, one of which at
least seems to be of questionable merit, a few
scattered articles spanning a generation, and
several doctoral dissertations comprise most of
the literature in English on Malebranche. A single translation of the _Entretiens_ _sur_ _la_ méta-
_physique_ _et_ _sur_ _la_ _religion_, executed in 1923 by
Morris Ginsberg, constitutes the only work of the
French Oratorian translated into English in recent
times.

This unfortunate state of affairs is rapidly
being remedied, however, by a vital resurgence
of interest in Malebranchian studies already
underway in France. This significant revival of
interest in Malebranche is due in large measure
to the indefatigible efforts of Henri Gouhier,
André Robinet, Geneviève Rodis-Lewis, Martial
Gueroult and Genette Dreyfus. Above all, however,
the recent publication of the critical edition of
the _Oeuvres_ _complètes_ _de_ _Malebranche_, under the
general editorship of André Robinet, finally makes
accessible a reliable and exhaustive instrument
for historically accurate studies of his thought.

ix

The significant feature of this renaissance of interest in the Oratorian's philosophy is that it is no longer primarily concerned, as were earlier studies, with Malebranche as a mere precursor of Berkeley, Hume or Kant, or as the successor of Descartes. Such studies, while important and instructive, tend all too often to destroy the integrity and obscure the consistency and coherence of his thought. Instead, the newer studies see Malebranche as a powerful thinker of original merit working out a new synthesis of philosophy and Christian theology which has contemporary significance in its own right.

The brief dialogue presented here for the first time in English is characteristic of Malebranche's lucidity of expression and depth of thought. It contains in abbreviated form the essence of his special brand of Cartesian metaphysics. Here it is expressed polemically against an ill-defined Chinese sage who, for Malebranche, represents all Neo-Confucians and, indeed, all atheists, as he understood the Chinese intellectuals of his day to be. The dialogue is not only philosophically illuminating but instructive also for a balanced historical understanding of the Cartesian movement after Descartes and before its demise in the eighteenth century.

Dominick A. Iorio

Rider College
Lawrenceville, New Jersey

# INTRODUCTION

Nicolas Malebranche was born in Paris exactly one month before Louis XIV on August 5, 1638 and died one month after the death of the Grand Monarch, on October 13, 1715. He was the last of thirteen children and was plagued throughout his youth with frail health and a fragile constitution. After pursuing philosophical studies at the Collège de La Marche (Paris), he attended the Sorbonne to study theology. Upon the death of his parents, he entered the novitiate of the Oratory at Paris in 1660. Within months of his ordination to the priesthood he was abruptly converted to Cartesianism in 1664, after chancing upon Descartes' de l'Homme.

His Recherche de la vérité (1674-76) was the first fruit of his reflections on mathematics and Cartesian philosophy, followed immediately by the Conversations chrétiennes (1676) and the Traité de la Nature et de la Grâce (1680). These were succeeded by the Méditations chrétiennes et métaphysique (1683), Traité de la morale (1684), and his classic Entretiens sur la métaphysique et sur la religion (1688). Numerous additional works and a prolific correspondence appeared in the course of a literary career that spanned more than forty years, frequently marked by sometimes bitter and acrimonious polemic exchanges with Antoine Arnauld of Port-Royale. Other correspondents included Wilhelm Leibniz, J.J. Dortous de Mairan, and Sylvain Regis. Eventually, broken in health, he died peacefully in 1715 at the age of seventy-seven.

It had been Malebranche's intention to work out a synthesis of Cartesian philosophy, Augustinian theology, and Christian revelation as a weapon against the emerging materialism, atheism, and ethical naturalism. Extremely popular during his life and for some time after his death, Malebranche was eventually overshadowed by Locke, Hume and Kant.

Malebranche was sixty-nine years old when in 1707 he undertook to write this uniquely significant work of his long and prolific literary career. Compared with his better known and more weighty opera, the Dialogue Between a Christian Philosopher and a Chinese Philosopher is both brief and hastily written. Yet for all its brevity and haste, it constitutes Malebranche's only effort to come to grips with the rather intense attention given to Oriental thought, specifically Chinese thought, by some of his contemporaries, including Leibniz.

Of particular interest is the fact that we have in this dialogue the only sustained encounter ever attempted to pit Cartesian philosophy by a major representative of that school against the alleged atheism of Confucian thought as understood in the late seventeenth and early eighteenth centuries. The fate of this polemic encounter is fascinating and instructive, both for the history of ideas and for the history of philosophy. Although some attention has been given to the scope of awareness and depth of understanding of Oriental thought in the seventeenth and eighteenth centuries by some European authors, precious little consideration has been devoted in America to this important aspect of the history of modern European philosophy.[1]

It is not the intention here to present a thorough review of such an extensive, though little explored, subject. Ours is the more modest effort to assess the peculiar manner utilized by Malebranche to interpret the thought of Chu-Hsi from the perspective of a well-developed and amplified Cartesianism in the service of religion. Malebranche's ostensible intention in writing this dialogue was to meet the specific needs of Catholic missionaries attempting to refute Chinese (Neo-Confucian) thought as they encountered it among the intellectuals they sought to convert in their far-flung Chinese mission fields.

The dialogue, however, serves still another

purpose, and one apparently unintended by Malebranche at the time he wrote it. The work became immediately popular within certain quarters while it was still in manuscript form. Its popularity engendered, as so many of his works had done previously, a violent debate between certain Jesuits and Dominicans which was felt from Rome to China. The debate concerned some concessions to Confucian rites granted by the Jesuits to their Chinese converts. We shall describe the debate and its merits below. Suffice it to say for now that the debate reveals an aspect of Malebranche's personality and literary life which throws into sharp relief both his own distaste for burdensome debates and the peculiar relations he had with many of his contemporaries who had simultaneously the highest respect for his writings and always a violent reaction to some aspect of them.

According to Yves Marie André, the outstanding and earliest biographer of the French Oratorian, the factors that led to the production of this work are as follows. While vacationing at the home of his intimate friend, Remond de Montmort, Malebranche had occasion to meet and hold lengthy conversations with Lartus de Lionne, Bishop of Rosalie. Both men were advanced in age and quickly developed a very close friendship full of mutual respect and admiration. Bishop de Lionne had recently returned to France from China, where he had spent twenty years as a missionary and where he had been instrumental in establishing a flourishing church. In their conversations the two would invariably discuss not only the work of the missions, but especially Chinese philosophy and religion and the difficulties faced by Christian missionaries in their tireless attempts to convince Chinese intellectuals of the defects in their philosophical and religious outlooks. Already familiar with Malebranche's work in philosophy, Bishop de Lionne asked his advice and begged him to help the missionaries in these endeavors by producing a brief work serviceable to the missionaries in China. Driven by charity and affection, Malebranche agreed to do so.

Although the idea of addressing himself to a philosophy totally alien to him was of no pressing interest to him in his old age, Malebranche nevertheless felt constrained to accede to the entreaties of his friend and promised a brief treatise on the existence and nature of God conformable to Bishop de Lionne's wishes. The work was rather hastily written during the summer of 1707 and began to circulate in manuscript form. At the time Malebranche had no intention of submitting the treatise to publication but simply sought to satisfy the request of his friend for an instrument to serve as a guide to Christian missionaries in their Chinese outposts.[2]

## The Rites Affair

The dialogue's appearance in manuscript form caught the attention of a number of individuals who avidly read the work not for the purpose for which it was intended, but rather as a contribution to a heated controversy usually referred to as "the Rites Affair."[3]

The controversy had its roots in the clash between the Jesuits, who prided themselves on being the first missionaries to China, and the Dominicans who contested this honor. Little was needed to stimulate the passions that accompanied the traditional rivalries characteristic of much of the history of the major religious orders in Europe. That stimulus was provided by the Jesuits themselves when Father Matthew Ricci, the Jesuit Superior in China, permitted or tolerated certain traditional Confucian rites to be practiced among the recent converts to Catholicism. While not all Jesuit missionaries agreed with such permissiveness, seeing it as a concession to superstition, tolerance was nevertheless shown to converts from Confucianism by a majority of these missionaries. Father Ricci's successor, Father Nicolo Longobardi, attempted strenuously to undo the damage inflicted by his predecessor, but to

4

no avail. He sought the same unequivocal condemnation of ritual practice against Confucianism
as was levied against Taoism and Buddhism, seeing
the former as no less idolatrous than the latter.

While the Jesuits debated the issue among themselves, a Dominican friar, Father Juan Bautista
Morales, entered China in 1631 accompanied by a
Franciscan friar, Father Antoine de Sainte-Marie.
In their journey through China they grew increas-
ingly shocked and alarmed at the idolatrous
practices they witnessed among the converted
Chinese. They were even more dismayed when they
learned that these practices were not only tolerated but openly permitted and even encouraged by
the Jesuits. Despite their remonstrances, they
received no satisfaction from their Jesuit confreres and turned instead to Rome to express their
indignation and to seek relief. Through the
efforts of Father Morales, Innocent X decreed in
1645 a condemnation of Confucian ceremonies, including among others the practice of ancestral
worship.

Bitten by the defeat suffered in Rome, several
Jesuit missionaries, under the leadership of
Father Martin Martini, pleaded the Jesuit case
before the Holy Office. They undoubtedly made am-
ply clear to the papal auditors the high degree of
success missionaries like Father Ricci experienced
when they assumed the dress and habits of the host
country, committed to memory the texts of Confucius, served a number of secular interests in
the political and scholarly life of China, and
made concessions to traditional Chinese ceremonies not totally antagonistic to proper Christian
conduct and belief. Thousands of Chinese had been
converted, sometimes in a single year, by pursuing
precisely these policies. The effect of their
pursuasive arguments was a decree in 1656 from
Alexander VII which contradicted in part the earlier decree of Innocent X. The issuance of two
contrary papal decrees served only to intensify
the debate. In 1669 Clement IX re-affirmed the
original decree. The embarrassment for all

parties was complete.

With everyone's honor at stake, Innocent XI in 1684 dispatched his own hand-picked Jesuit dele-gates to China who were neutrals in the debate and respected by all parties.  These included Father J. F. Fouquet and Father Claude de Visdelou as Apostolic Vicars.  As a result of their in-vestigations, the Jesuit policies and practices were condemned as supporting idolatry.  Despite repeated objections to the findings of the Apostolic Vicars and exhaustive defenses of the Jesuit policies still in force, Clement XI issued a decree condemning the practices absolutely and declaring the matter closed.  Unrelentingly, the Jesuits continued to appeal this final decision of the Pope both in China and before the public in France and elsewhere.

It is at this juncture in the debate that Male-branche's manuscript made its appearance.  It was inevitable, under the circumstances of time and place, that the work would be construed as an at-tempt on the Oratorian's part to enter the con-troversy on the side of the Dominicans and against the Jesuits.  The invective levelled at Malebranche because of this suspicion was extremely bitter. His biographer and friend, Father André (himself a Jesuit) complained that the Jesuits appeared to assign the most ignorant of their professors to refute Malebranche and that these critics succeed-ed only in presenting themselves as insolent, stupid pedants.[4]  The Jesuits, in fact, went so far as to solicit the Holy Office to have his works placed on the Index.

A gentle and modest man, Malebranche had through all of this refused to accede to the demands of his friends that he publish the Dialogue, since he did not wish to fuel the flames of dissension and vilification which involved even his friends, in-cluding Father André.  However, even this decision was taken out of his hands when a critique of his work appeared in the Jesuit Mémoires de Trévoux in July of 1708 written by Father Louis Marquer.  The review was poorly executed, replete with untruths and misreadings, full of calumny against Malebranche, and insolent in tone. To set the record straight Malebranche decided to publish the <u>Dialogue</u>, appending to it a preface responding point by point to his detractor. His defense was mild but effective, noting the errors, calumnies and lack of understanding manifested by the author of the review.

A second Jesuit review appeared in the <u>Mémoires</u> in December of the same year replete with arguments against the philosophy of the Oratorian, arguments drawn from earlier criticisms made more effectively by Antoine Arnauld. Tired of repeating his rebuttals to the criticisms of Arnauld, which had been published extensively years before, and being in ill health and close to death, Malebranche decided to issue his <u>Recueil</u> de <u>toute le réponses à</u> M. <u>Arnauld</u> (1709), his last major response to all objections and to all objectors. The matter, unfortunately, did not end even with Malebranche's death in 1715, as evidenced by a letter from Leibniz concerning Chinese philosophy to Malebranche's friend, Remond, in 1716. In this lengthy letter Leibniz pleads for a genuine appraisal of Chinese philosophy, and with Malebranche clearly in mind, warns against some misunderstandings of that philosophy recently published and receiving wide attention.[5]

It would not be accurate to say that Malebranche was unwittingly drawn into the Rites Affair. Surely he must have been sufficiently aware of the debate taking place for some years between the Jesuits and the Dominicans, if not from his days at the Sorbonne and at the Collège de la Marche, then certainly from his conversations with Bishop de Lionne. The Oratorian must have seen that, unappealing as such an undertaking was so late in life, the preparation of the new work requested by his friend could be used effectively to serve some purposes he himself undoubtedly must have had in mind.

A deeply spiritual man, jealous for the purity
of his own religious faith and practice and anx-
ious to maintain its integrity, he was offended
by the Jesuits' efforts to convert the world to
Christianity by opportunistic and truth-debasing
means. But of more immediate concern to him was
in all probability the fact that his arch-critic,
Antoine Arnauld, was now dead and that here was an
opportunity to respond anew to some of the objections raised by Arnauld in works published
since his death. The criticisms of Arnauld had
been presented over a forty-year period, beginning with Arnauld's critique of Malebranche's
first publication, the Recherche de la vérité in
1668. The most biting criticism Malebranche had
to contend with was Arnauld's often-repeated
charge that the Oratorian's philosophy was fundamentally no different in its principles and consequences from that of the infamous Spinoza, who
also sought to identify infinite extension with
the essence of God. When, therefore, it was pointed out by Bishop de Lionne and others that Confucianism was fundamentally a form of atheism and
a kind of Spinozism, it is little wonder that Malebranche saw the advantage of establishing one more
time and for the last time the difference between
his philosophy and the "atheism" of Spinoza, dis-
guised as Confucianism. It seems justifiable to
assert that these were the probable factors that
induced Malebranche to write the dialogue, even
though it meant sustaining the ferocity of Jesuit
indignation. Arnauld's charge over the years had
stung and hurt him deeply. The two had been fair-
ly close friends before the charge was initially
levelled. Malebranche, who had something of the
mystic in him---and certainly something of the
idealist---recoiled from the charge of Spinozism
precisely because in his own mind Spinozism meant
nothing more than an atheism of the worst kind,
the reduction of God to matter. To deny the existence of God outright may be ascribed to ignorance. To identify God with matter, on the other
hand, implies a perfidious denial of the spiritual
which involves a perversity of soul. This, at
least, was how Malebranche understood Spinoza.

# The Philosophy of Malebranche

In his first major work, <u>Recherche</u> <u>de</u> <u>la</u> <u>vérité</u>, Malebranche begins his search for the truth by means of an investigation of the causes of deception and error and attempts to articulate the right method of arriving at truth. Only error, he claims, causes our wretchedness and the evil we find in the world. It is the worm in our being which must be eliminated at any cost, if we are ever to satisfy our constant hope for true happiness. This happiness can only be attained if we strive to restore the original and natural relation we have to God rather than to body. The relation of our souls to God is more natural and more intimate than our soul's connection with the body. The metaphysical source of error in our lives is to be found in the ruptured union of our souls with God, in our undue dependence on our bodies and, through them, to the world of sensation and dependence upon the material world. But although our connection with God is somewhat confused and only dimly perceived, it is nevertheless real and basic to our being. We are God-related creatures who must come to understand that relationship and submit to its demands.[6]

At the outset Malebranche lays down a general rule to be followed in the quest for truth, namely, that "we should never give a complete assent save to things that we see evidently."[7] Directing his attention first to the senses, he argues against the sceptics that it is not the senses which deceive us, but rather it is our will which deceives us by its precipitous judgments. All too frequently our wills show remarkable haste in consenting to an apparent agreement between the relation of things to us and the nature of things themselves. There is nothing wrong in consenting to the judgment that I feel warm, but error follows when I affirm that the warmth I feel is outside of my experience of it. The same may be said of all secondary qualities, as Descartes noted earlier. We should, therefore, never confuse things in themselves and our perceptions of them

9

and assent to a judgment which identifies their relation to us with their objective nature. The senses cannot reveal to us what bodies are in themselves, but they are reliable and exact when they inform us of the relations bodies have with our own bodies. Proper use of them, therefore, conserves health and life, a function for which they are admirably suited.

What has been argued with regard to sense perception may be similarly argued in the case of the imagination. As a power to produce or reproduce images of material things, it is no more geared to instruct us about the objective character of material beings than the senses themselves are. Both sense and imagination are rooted in the character and constitution of the body, so that their errors can be exposed only by means of a meticulous analysis of the dependence of the soul on the body and the peculiar ways in which the body works when it is sensing and imagining. These analyses are executed by Malebranche with consummate skill and painstaking attention to the minutest details of physiological processes based in large measure on Descartes' mechanistic principles of physiology.

It is only when we turn to the pure understanding, to mind in its spiritual purity, that we are able to know with clarity and metaphysical certainty all there is to know about bodies and to attain to whatever truth is accessible to us about our own souls and about God. But truth is attainable only if we recognize the finite, and therefore limited, capacity of the mind and pursue a right method for the attainment of truth and the avoidance of error.

The principal rule of this method is that we must reason only on those matters about which we have clear ideas, as Descartes noted, proceeding from the simple to the most complex. But what is the nature and source of our ideas?

For Malebranche an idea is whatever represents some object to the mind, whether clearly or confusedly, or, what is the immediate object of the mind. In its most precise signification an idea is to be understood as that which represents things to the mind in a manner so clear that one may intuitively (par une simple vue) grasp precisely what modifications actually belong to it. Malebranche claims that in its purity mind or understanding is to be distinguished from ideas in the strict sense. Thus, while understanding is the power possessed by the mind to know objects outside itself, ideas are the means by which it perceives extra-mental objects.[8] The power called understanding is for him a purely passive capacity, a receptivity in relation to knowledge. When it receives its object it is then illuminated. Its immediate object is an idea, an intelligibility which activates the understanding.

What then is the source of these ideas or intelligibilities? According to the French Oratorian, there are five possible sources which need to be considered: (1) ideas come from bodies; or (2) our soul has the power to produce them; or (3) God produces them with the creation of the soul, or at least He produces them in the soul each time it thinks of some object; or (4) the soul possesses all the perfections it sees in bodies; or (5) the soul sees all things in God. Malebranche proceeds systematically to eliminate the first four possible sources, clarifying as he does so how ideas are to be understood and how each succeeding position has greater reasonableness than the preceding. We have here a kind of Platonic ascent of the soul to a wider vision and better grasp of the truth with each step taken, or more precisely, a preparation of the soul for a more adequate vision of truth.[9] We are gradually brought into the presence of ideas as these are seen intuitively in God.

Malebranche prepares his readers for the acceptance of the theory of the vision in God by attacking as a possible source of our ideas the view still popular in his day that we possess in

ourselves the impressed species of sensible things
and that these species are abstracted by the Agent
Intellect and received by the Passive Intellect
where they become spiritualized and expressed.
Malebranche shows little patience with, or sym-
pathy for, what he claims is a pretentious "Peripatetic" opinion which lacks all solid foundation.[10]

It is in his appraisal of the second theory
(that man's soul has the power to produce ideas)
that Malebranche seriously attacks the Peripatetic
theory of ideas. In this theory, which he claims
is more sophisticated than the first, our souls
are viewed as having the power to produce ideas
either at will or on the occasion that they are
stimulated to do so by the impressions made on our
bodies by external objects. He strongly condemns
this position as pretentious and presumptuous.
Ideas are real, spiritual beings with real properties. They are radically distinct and different
from the bodies they represent. Because of this
special character they are more noble than bodies.
In fact, the entire intelligible world is superior
in its perfection to the material world. If it
were in the power of men to produce ideas, they
would have power to create a world more noble and
more perfect than God himself created. In fact,
their power would be greater even than God's in
that it is much harder to produce something spiritual from matter and motion, which contribute nothing to its production, than to create something
from nothing. Such a theory, therefore, involves
itself in metaphysical absurdities and results
from the "ignorance and vanity" of man. Once we
grant reality to ideas, the production of them by
the mind becomes a matter of creation. But even
if this power were granted to man, for the sake of
argument, how would he be able to use it? Man can
no more will an idea he has not known a priori
than a painter can paint an animal he has never
seen. So that either we already possess the idea
and therefore know it, or we lack the idea al-
together and do not know it. If we already know
it, it is vain to create another; if we do not

know it, it is impossible to will what we do not already know. Malebranche has here prepared the ground for the third alternative possibility, namely, that our ideas are innate. Malebranche rightly understood that if man's soul could produce ideas out of itself this could be possible only on the assumption that the soul already possesses the ideas for which such a theory seeks to account.

His detailed attack upon the Peripatetic position implies that only God can create the intelligible world, the implication being that this intelligible world, as real and spiritual, is somehow in God. Further implied in his critique of the Aristotelians, and in agreement with them, is that concrete things, such as a horse or a man, cannot be spontaneously produced by the mind but must first be apprehended in sensation. However, if this sense content is to be understood at all, it is the pure understanding which alone can know its intelligibility. On the other hand, if the understanding is to grasp the intelligibility of what is presented to sense, it must of necessity already possess, a priori, the perfect ideas which represent these sensible objects. It is, therefore, the source of these ideas already in the mind that must be discovered. It would appear, consequently, that a doctrine of innate ideas, such as propounded by Descartes, is more acceptable than the Aristotelian theory so widely held among his contemporaries.

The theory of innate ideas, however, is itself subject to serious objections. To be sure it does not imply any corruption of the mind or any intellectual vice as so many other doctrines do; but if this theory were true, we would have to maintain that God created with each soul an infinity of infinite numbers of ideas, an absurdity which does violence to reason. This would be the case especially because we can conceive not only an infinity of simple geometrical figures belonging to, let us say, the class of polygons, but also an infinity of classes of different figures. While it is true that we cannot comprehend the infinite, we can nevertheless conceive it and understand that it is a system of relations and the connections of relations. Hence, it can at least be conceived by us all at once, although it can never be comprehended all at once by any finite mind. In other words, even granting that God is powerful enough to have created an infinity of ideas in each mind, still it is unreasonable to assume that God acted in this manner, since he is able to act more simply, easily and directly than in this cumbersome manner. A more economical hypothesis is, therefore, preferable to innatism.

The theory of innate ideas has one defect that it shares with the Peripatetic view that the mind creates ideas. Assuming that our minds possessed a store-house of all ideas, it would still be impossible to explain how the mind could elicit from this store-house the correct ideas to represent everything it sees when we suddenly open our eyes in a field, for example. Obviously, no sensible image resembles our idea of the sun; therefore, we would find it impossible to explain how the mind can select the one correct idea needed to represent this sun according to this size and shape and brilliance. In short, the theory of innate ideas fails utterly to explain how we are able to see objects in our environment.

One of the merits of the theory, nevertheless, is its recognition that ideas are always present to us, since we can will to think them at any time. Further, we would not be in a position to see anything were the idea not already present to us and in us, if only in a confused manner. But although for Malebranche ideas reside in us and their presence is confusedly felt, they are in no sense modifications of the soul as Descartes claimed they were. For the Oratorian the immediate object of our mind is "rien de crée."[11] This should be obvious since we can think of indeterminate being, of a circle in general, or of immense spaces, characteristics which are lacking in created beings which are neither infinite nor general. The implication in the innatist theory of Descartes is that the mind embraces the material world in some eminent manner, so that one might argue that the soul sees things outside itself by means of an inspection of its own perfections. But Malebranche refuses to accept this position. It is true that the soul grasps without benefit of ideas its own modifications, but it cannot perceive the essence nor the existence of outside objects simply by consulting itself. Ideas are not modifications of the soul. This view of Descartes would have the soul be the intelligible world which comprehends within itself everything included in the material and sensible world. But for the Oratorian this is vanity sprung from a love of independence and a desire to resemble God on the part of the fallen creature. The intelligible world is to be found in God alone, since he had the ideas of all things in creating them. These ideas are none other than God himself, so that the ideas of all things---even the most material---are to be found only in God, albeit in a spiritual manner. Malebranche's position is unequivocally stated. The ideas God has of things are not at all different from God himself, he claims; and even the most material and terrestrial creatures are contained in God in a manner that is completely spiritual but incomprehensible to us.[12] It is in his own essence, therefore, that God sees the essence of all things insofar as they are contained in him. Their existence in turn is seen in the eternal decrees of his will. The obvious conclusion is, therefore, that if ideas are not innate to us and if these ideas are found only in God, then granted we do see the essences of things which are always present to us, it follows that we see all things only in God. As Malebranche declares in the first lines of the Preface to the Recherche de la vérité, the mind of man is more intimately united to God than to the body; and this union with God is natural, necessary and absolutely indispensable to the mind.[13]

The purpose of the vast argumentation which culminates in the famous theory of the vision in God is two-fold: (a) to determine the source of our

ideas, and (b) to determine their residency or
ontological status.  The conclusions Malebranche
draws along the way constitute the foundation
stones of his entire philosophical edifice.  Thus,
it is certain for him that bodies are not visible
in themselves and that to know objects we must be
united to them in some manner.  Given, however,
the radical distinction between soul and body, we
can know bodies only by means of ideas which represent them.  These representative ideas are
universal and a priori to experience, although
not innate in Descartes' sense of the term. Furthermore, these ideas are real beings, spiritual in
character and uncreated.  As such they are superi-
or to the soul and exist independently of the
soul.  Nevertheless, ideas are always present to
the soul but are not modifications of the soul.
These ideas, in their totality, constitute an intelligible world which is infinite and which re-
sides only in God.  Hence, since we are united to
this intelligible world immediately, we must conclude that whatever we know we see immediately and
only in God.  However, although this last conclusion is clearly indicated, it must be elaborated
"pour la bien comprendre."

The strongest argument for the theory of the
vision in God is drawn from the manner in which
the mind perceives all things.  Experience shows
that when we desire to consider some particular object we first of all grasp in a confused and general manner all beings.  It is impossible to direct our attention to one object unless we already
know it, albeit in a confused and general way.  It
is this a priori grasp of all beings that allows
us to shift our attention explicitly now to this
particular object and now to that.  This could not
be possible were the ideas of all beings not already present to our minds, which is to say, were
we not united to God who embraces the intelligible
world in himself.  It is this union with God which
also gives us a grasp of all beings as included in
one, so that we can represent universal ideas and
thereby know abstract and general truths.14

Related to this experience of the a priori presence in our souls of all beings is the presence to our minds of the idea of the Infinite which gives us a very distinct idea of God as infinitely perfect being. This idea, which we perceive but do not comprehend, is had by us even before the idea of the finite. Being-as-being is grasped initially as unlimited, and only after this general notion is abridged do we conceive a finite being. In fact, for Malebranche the mind is incapable of perceiving or thinking about anything except within and through the idea it always possesses and has ever before it of the infinite.[15] The idea of the infinite, furthermore, is not to be understood as a mere assemblage of particular beings; instead, particular ideas are to be understood as participations of this idea. The infinite is, in fact, the being of God himself acting on our understanding. Truth is uncreated, immutable, immense and eternal---it is God himself. Hence, we see God. But it is not the substance of God that we see, but rather the ideas of material and sensible things which represent them. All these ideas, an "infinite infinity" of them, reside in God and are comprehended in the simplicity of God's being in a manner which is to us incomprehensible.

## Arnauld and the Charge of Spinozism

In response to certain objections raised by critics regarding the placing in God of an infinity of particular ideas, Malebranche introduced in the $X^e$ Eclaircissement to the Recherche de la vérité the notion of "intelligible extension" which contains within itself the ideas of all possible modes of extension. This ordered hierarchy of intelligibilities (essences) is then posited in God, but not as a modification of God's substance. However, in the opening sentence of the fifteenth chapter of the Livre de vraies et des fausses idées Antoine Arnauld asserts that there is nothing less intelligible than intelligible extension.[16] With this statement Arnauld initiates an explicit attack at

17

the root of the doctrine of the vision in God and of Malebranche's theory of knowledge. He realized that Malebranche's entire position with respect to knowledge of bodies and hence his theory of ideas rested on the notion of intelligible extension. His initial attack is from two directions: (1) despite his introduction of the notion of intelligible extension, one may still inquire of Malebranche if there is not a plurality of particular ideas in God; and (2) Malebranche fails to show how this idea is related to God, so that in effect he introduces more confusion into the discussion of knowledge than there would be without this notion.

In reply to the first objection, Malebranche simply refers Arnauld back to the Recherche de la vérité and to the Eclaircissements, claiming that Arnauld had misunderstood him or not read him closely enough.[17] The more serious criticism, however, concerned the status of the notion of intelligible extension in God. To the question regarding whether intelligible extension is or is not a creature, Malebranche answers that it is a creature in the sense that God created extension. But, demands Arnauld, is created extension God or in God? It is God himself, responded Malebranche, but only as participable by creatures. But, urged Arnauld, if intelligible extension is not only found in God but is God and at the same time is the essence of body and representative of bodies, then Malebranche is inescapably rendering God corporeal. The Oratorian must have known and intended to place in God real extension and not a so-called intelligible extension.[18] The conclusion Arnauld was seeking is not difficult to discern, although the specific charge is made for the first time in his Défense de M. Arnauld, namely, that the Oratorian has propounded a position which leads unequivocally and inexorably to that of Spinoza.[19]

In his Méditations chrétiennes et métaphysiques (1683) Malebranche takes great pains to differentiate his own position from that of "le misérable Spinoza."[20] The charge of Spinozism not only

larmed him but angered him as well.[21]  In the
ninth Meditation to the above work he takes up
the question of creation and declares that philosophers (Spinoza?) are "stupides et ridicules"
when they deny the possibility of creation simply
because they cannot conceive that God's power is
great enough to make something from nothing.  Yet,
they do not hesitate to affirm that God can move
a straw.  But if they take sufficient care, they
will find that they are no more able to conceive
the latter activity than they are the former, since
they lack any clear idea of efficacy or of power.
Nevertheless, it is possible to prove that matter
is not uncreated.  If matter were uncreated, God
would have no power over it, because he can act on
it only if he knows it.  He cannot know matter unless he gives it existence, for he can have only
that knowledge which is drawn from himself alone.
It is certain, besides, that nothing can act on God
or illuminate him; rather, it is he who acts and
illuminates.  Since God can move bodies, he created them.  Any other conclusion would deny God's
existence by rendering him ignorant and impotent.[22]
Further, if matter were uncreated it would be
immobile.  Bodies can move only through the agency
which gives them being.  Their action is due to
their causa essendi which wills their existence in
successive and different places or in the same place
at the same or different moments of time. Creation, conservation, and motion are all the same
activity.[23]  All power and efficacy are from God
alone.  This is the basis for Malebranche's oc-
casionalism.

There is, however, another reason why some deny
that matter is created.  The thought of extension
leads them to regard it as a necessary being.
They fail to realize that they are in fact imagining the world as created in immense spaces
which had no beginning and which God himself is
powerless to destroy.  This is to confuse matter,
the existent, with intelligible spaces, the non-
existent.  There are two species of extension, intelligible and material.  The former is eternal,
immense, necessary.  It is the immensity of God

19

both as participable by creatures (corporeal bodies)
and as representative of an immense matter. It is
the intelligible idea of an infinity of possible
worlds. Intelligible extension is what we con-
template whenever we think of the infinite.

Material extension, on the other hand, is the
matter of which the world is composed; it is in-
visible and unable to act on our minds. It is con-
tingent, limited and created. It is a serious
error, he argues, to confuse this kind of extension with intelligible extension. Such a confusion
easily results when we judge beyond what is actually contained in the idea itself of extension.
This is the error of Spinoza, confusing the ideas
of things created by God with things themselves,
or, intelligible extension with material extension.[24] His refusal to accept the notion of creation led Spinoza, according to Malebranche, to
reject the distinction between these two types of
extension.

Had Spinoza been alive to respond to these objections and positions, he would probably have
referred Malebranche to his anti-creationist arguments in the Ethics,[25] in which he claims that all
creationist arguments contain a basic fallacy.
They all assume that extension is composed of parts
At the same time they refer to extension as a substance. If the attributes of substance were divisible, the divided parts would either retain the
nature of substance, as Spinoza understood it, or
they would not. If they were to retain this nature
they would be themselves infinite and self-caused
and would thereby be other substances. But since
a substance itself is not divisible,[26] there can
be only one substance.[27] If, on the other hand,
the divided parts do not retain the nature of substance, then the whole substance would cease to be
a substance, assuming it were wholly divided. This
is unacceptable, because substance by nature exists and cannot cease to exist.[28] The only conclusion to be drawn is that substance cannot be
divided. The arguments of the adversaries, whom

does not name, have cogency only because, in
tempting to demonstrate that extended substance
finite, they assume that an infinite extension
measurable and composed of parts which are
nite. In effect what they are doing is arguing
a circle. To show that extended substance is
nite, they claim it is composed of finite parts
d therefore measurable by means of division.
is renders extended substances passive and there-
re finite. Since for Spinoza the proper notion
extended substance is that of infinity, unity and indivisibility, any idea of extension
ich does not include these notes is inadmis-
ble.[29]

It is seriously questionable whether Malebranche
ally understood what Spinoza meant by calling God
extended being. It is apparently true that
lebranche was not well acquainted with the phil-
ophy of Spinoza. He seems to have been inter-
ted in Spinoza's philosophy only to the extent
at he thought he recognized in it the source of
resy,[30] and admitted to J.J. Dortous de Mairan
at he read Spinoza only briefly.[31] Regardless
the level of understanding, however, it seems
ear that Malebranche not only did not answer
tisfactorily Arnauld's objections but did not
equately refute the charge of Spinozism.

To clear himself completely of this association
th Spinoza two serious questions had to be an-
ered without equivocation: (1) what precisely is
e relation of intelligible extension to God; and
) how are intelligible extension and material
reated) extension related? Both problems, we
ght mention parenthetically, vexed the Oratorian
the end of his life; and it must be confessed
at Malebranche's evasive language from one work
another and from one edition to another of the
me work make a final determination of his posi-
on well nigh impossible.

Dortous de Mairan appears to have noted as late
1714 that Malebranche's response to Arnauld's

charges were not entirely clear or consistent. The distinction between intelligible extension and created extension, he seems to feel, had not been sufficiently clarified. The exact relation between the substance of God and intelligible extension was no less obscurely treated. At one time, declares Dortous de Mairan, intelligible extension seems to be the substance of God. At another time it seems to be an attribute. On occasion God's substance is even referred to as an extended substance. Bodies in turn are seen now as modifications or modes of created extension, which in turn seems to be a modification of intelligible extension, or of the Divine extended substance. How, asks Mairan, does all this differ from Spinoza?[32]

Apparently fed up with the constant accusations Malebranche calls Mairan's attention to a basic difference in the kind of extension, namely, a difference between essence and existence. Faith alone reveals to us the existence of the world of matter intelligible extension suffices to give us its essence. This intelligible extension is the essence of the world (created matter) whether that world exists or not. Bodies cannot act on mind. Only intelligible extension can affect the mind, since it alone is efficacious.[33]

Mairan, however, was not fully convinced that the distinction made by the Oratorian settled the questions he had raised. One of his objections remained, namely, that one part of extension cannot differ from any other part of it, since the parts of extension can be distinguished neither by accident nor by themselves, that is, by an internal difference. How, asks Mairan, can two pearls differ if they are not two distinct substances or at least modifications of a single substance? If, in other words, there is nothing internal to them which distinguishes one from the other, and nothing external to them which enables a distinction to be made, then it is absurd to affirm that they are in fact distinct. We should be unable to conceive how they can be distinct.

Malebranche's reply to this objection is that
he well understands that one cubic foot of extension is of the same nature as any other extension,
but the single factor that makes one cubic foot
of extension different from all others is its existence.  Existence, therefore, and not essence is
the principle of individuation for Malebranche. It
is existence which appears to give concretion to
essence considered as the figure of the thing.
Whereas figure limits extension, existence limits
the infinity of figure by making it this figure
and no other.  In light of the fact that for Malebranche we know of the existence of the material
world only by faith and never by way of experience,
his answer seems to be of dubious value.  Since we
do not grasp the existence of things in experience
and yet have an experience of individuals, it
would seem that the principle of individuation must
be sought in something other than existence alone.

In a final letter to Mairan, who always remained sceptical, Malebranche repeated himself in
seeming desperation by a summary statement of his
central positions articulated innumerable times
before in the course of more than a generation.[34]


Malebranche and Neo-Confucianism

Malebranche did not have a particular Chinese
philosopher in mind in the preparation of this
dialogue.  Rather, he was interested in addressing
himself to a deeply rooted tradition in China ex-
tending back to Confucius and Mencius.  More specifically, he understood Chinese philosophy (apart
from Taoist and Buddhist currents) to be charact-
erized by a Neo-Confucian tradition whose chief
exponent was Chu-Hsi (1130-1200), "probably the
greatest synthesizer in the history of Chinese
thought."[35]  It was Chu-Hsi who welded the di-
vergent forms of Neo-Confucianism, whether ideal-
ist or rationalist, metaphysical or moral, into a
single, comprehensive system grounded in the
classics of Confucianism on the one hand and on a

thoroughly explicated metaphysics on the other. His doctrine of the Great Ultimate and his resolution of the problem of how Jen (humanity) is to be cultivated and perfected sufficed to render his the orthodox interpretation of Confucianism from his time to ours.

The central problem Chu-Hsi attempted to resolve concerned the relation between good and evil, or more precisely, how to reconcile the basic goodness of human nature with the reality of moral evil and ignorance. This he accomplished by drawing a distinction between man's original nature, which is good, and man's actual nature, as it is embodied in material force (ch'i). This force or matter (Ether) gives to every being its substance and form. To make these notions clearer, however, it is necessary to understand Chu-Hsi's notion of the Great Ultimate, the Li referred to in Malebranche's dialogue.

The Great Ultimate is nothing more than principle.[36] As such, it is subsistent and transcends space and time, as well as the categories of existence and non-existence. Existence is a "resting place" of principle, a determination of it. The Great Ultimate, however, is undetermined to be or not to be. Put differently, as principle the Great Ultimate is indifferent or neutral with regard to being and non-being. All categories of thought and being are strictly inapplicable to it, whether of time, space, place, motion, existence or non-existence. Each of these categories involves Li, for the Great Ultimate is in each thing in its entirety. The Li is wrongly understood if it is apprehended as being incarnated in things in such a way that a part of it is in one thing and another part of it is in another. Rather, without being exhausted, it is in its entirety incarnated or concretized in each and every thing, category, attribute, modification, habit and so on. Things, ideas, possibilities, whatever can be or be conceived participate in the Great Ultimate. The myriad are the one and the one is the myriad. Each individual existent is part

24

of the Great Ultimate. But just as the moon is not fractured when its light is shared by moonlit objects, so also the Great Ultimate is not fragmented or scattered by this great sharing.[37] It remains always and only what it is.

When Chu-Hsi declares that the Great Ultimate is the totality of myriad things, he does not mean that the totality of existents literally constitutes the Great Ultimate. Rather, because nothing can be in any sense without principle, so that each existent has a particular principle (li) which makes it be and be what it is (essence), it is the principles (essences) of all things that may be termed the Great Ultimate. In other words, the sum total of inner intelligible contents of all that exists or can be conceived constitutes in its intelligible unity the Great Ultimate, the principle of all principles, the essence of essence. The name itself is simply an appellation for what is fundamentally beyond all naming.[38]

In the Dialogue Malebranche seems to understand the Li and matter to be essentially identical. While logically distinct, they are ontologically the same. He seems therefore to construe the Great Ultimate as the being of the world, the total assemblage of things. This is why Confucians were conceived popularly as idolators and gross pantheists and why Malebranche was able to make an easy identification of Neo-Confucianism with Spinozism. Yet, for Chu-Hsi the Great Ultimate is not only a transcendent reality, it is the only transcendent reality. The most that can be said of it amounts to little else than "vague description." Each human being must arrive at a personal realization of the truth.[39]

But there is for Chu-Hsi a realm of reality that can be more easily described; this is the world "within shapes," a world formed by the action of the Ether (ch'i) or matter. Formed by and set in motion by the principles of Yin and Yang, matter became compressed to form an undifferentiated chaos consisting initially of only fire and water.

25

The water gradually hardened, according to fixed
principles, while fire became dissipated and
formed the celestial regions, in addition to becoming wind and lightning on the earth itself.[40]

It is when essence (li) and matter combine
that things are formed as existing entities. The
same is true also of man.  The integration of
essence and material force gives birth to man.[41]
Death, then, is the disintegration of essence and
matter, but the essence or principle does not
persist in separation from matter nor the matter
from the essence.  The essence "returns to Heav-
en," that is, to a state of pure principle, while
matter "returns to Earth," that is, to a state of
pure potentially for a new integration with essence.  Neither essence nor matter can exist in
separation as substantial beings.  They are always
and only found co-existentially related, although
principle is logically prior to material force.
All of this, of course, sounds remarkably similar
to Aristotle's theory of hylomorphism, and were
not such a comparison outside the scope of this
brief essay it might be pursued with profit.

It is in these metaphysical considerations that
we encounter the foundation for Chu-Hsi's analysis
of human nature and his treatment of the problem
of moral evil.  Principle-as-such is good. In
fact, the Great Ultimate is the highest good, the
ultimate principle of goodness in all things, including man, comparable in some respects to Plato's
idea of the Good.  But although the Great Ultimate
is received by each nature in its entirety, it is
nevertheless constrained in its manifestation by
the imperfections and limitations of the recipient,
that is, corporeal matter.  A dog will by nature
manifest principle more restrictedly than a man
will.  Each will reflect principle only to the extent that the Great Ultimate can be exhibited or
expressed as dog or man and nothing else.  This
imperfect, yet unavoidable participation makes for
diversity and multiplicity, but it also makes for
limitation, imperfection, defectiveness, and evil.

26

...e actualization of principle necessarily in-
...lves imperfection, just as the drawn circle
...n never perfectly represent or concretize the
...eal circle, whose perfection is found only in
...s essential definition, or in that to which the
...finition refers. Men, likewise, are like so
...ny drawn circles, each basically good insofar as
...ch conforms to or incarnates the principle of
...n, but each also more or less imperfect and
...erefore subject to evil. Like a pearl immersed
...unclear water, man's nature, originally pure
...d clear, is immersed in matter so that its
...ster is not apparent.[42] But like a pearl, hu-
...n nature, though sullied by its immersion in
...tter, can be restored to its original luster by
...e practice of the specific virtues of love or
...manity (jen), righteousness (yi), propriety
...i), and wisdom (chih).

It is interesting to note that Malebranche
...es not address himself at all to the details of
...u-Hsi's metaphysical system and only superfi-
...ally to his moral teachings. He does not, for
...ample, indicate any awareness or interest in the
...lation of the Li to the principles of Ying and
...ng, or to the relation of Li to Ether and na-
...re. He is not concerned in any direct manner
...th Chu-Hsi's primary concern with the problem
...good and evil, although he touches on this
...oblem in the dialogue in the context of his own
...derstanding of the problem as a Cartesian. In-
...ead, Malebranche concentrates his attention on
...sentially one major facet of that philosophy,
...at is, on the general relation of the Li to the
...terial world, seeing the Li as essentially
...entified ontologically with matter, although
...gically distinguishable. In this sense, he
...entifies Chu-Hsi with his own understanding of
...inoza. In short, he construes Neo-Confucianism
...a Spinozistic monism and atheism and then uses
...at understanding to differentiate his own posi-
...on from that of Spinoza.

The Dialogue begins with a comparison between

Malebranche's understanding of the Li as the supreme law, truth and wisdom of the universe and
the personal God of Christianity, the incomprehensible Infinite. The God he proclaims, declares
Malebranche, is none other than the one whose idea
is already in us and present to our minds in a con
fused manner. He is not the anthropomorphic god
of popular Confucianism but the He Who Is of the
Sacred Scriptures. He then offers a proof of the
existence of the Christian God by an elucidation
of the idea of the infinite, acknowledging that
Neo-Confucians do not accept the infinite in any
existential sense. His demonstration of God's
existence, he contends, is "the most simple" of
any that can be given. To think at all is to
think being. More precisely put, what is immediately and directly before the mind when it is
actively thinking is real or exists. When, therefore, the mind thinks infinite being such a being
must exist. The mind is certainly not thinking
nothing when it thinks infinite being, for to
think nothing and not to think at all are the same
thing.

Following Descartes, Malebranche distinguishes
between formal and objective reality. As modes of
consciousness all ideas are alike for Descartes;
but as representative images they are diverse.
This diversity is due to the objective reality
found in each idea, that is, that objective content to which the idea, as a mental mode, refers.
An idea is a presence in me, a mental state like
any other idea. But what this idea is about is
its objective reality. When clearly and distinctly apprehended or understood such an idea is always true; it is precisely what it means or in-
tends, neither more nor less. In this sense every
idea, as a pure intelligible content, is a real
being; it has an ontological status. Formal reality, on the other hand, refers to what exists
extra-mentally and, indeed, apart from any idea,
such as a material body. The idea of a material
body will then be the intelligibility of the formal reality (the material body) which accounts for

e idea which represents it. Since there must be
certain parity between cause and effect, so that
e more perfect cannot be the effect of the less
erfect, it is impossible for any finite formal
eality to account for an infinite objective re-
lity. Only the formal reality God, understood
s infinite being, can account for the objective
eality of the innate idea of infinite being which
alebranche alleges we are all vaguely aware of
enever our minds are active.

Since the Chinese philosopher of the dialogue
s not persuaded by the argument drawn from the
dea of the infinite, Malebranche turns to an
pistemological analysis of the inaccessibility
f bodies to direct perception by the soul and
ncludes to his famous theory that we comprehend
ll things by "seeing" them in God's essence. To
larify this theory of the vision in God, the
ratorian seeks to reduce his opponent to silence
y elaborating the Cartesian notion of the reality
nd efficacy of ideas and the relationship of the
ind to the body, understanding both to be two
adically distinct realities. This discussion
esults in a concession by the Chinese philosopher
hat matter cannot think and that only the mind or
oul can. Once this is granted, Malebranche pro-
eeds to demonstrate (contrary to Descartes) that
here are no innate ideas in the soul and that, as
ntelligibles, all ideas must be found only in the
upreme Intelligible, God himself, understood not
nly as an abstract Wisdom, such as the Li, but
lso as a living, wise being fully conscious of
hat he does and why he orders beings as he does.
his natural order fixed by God is always drawn
rom God's own wisdom and is therefore good, both
etaphysically and morally.

How, then, argues the Chinese philosopher, does
alebranche explain the presence of evil in an all
ood universe? Surely, the reality of evil proves
here can be no beneficent God? Malebranche an-
wers like a good Cartesian that because our minds
re finite, we do not know the diverse ends or the
otal design of the universe; and we are therefore

not in a position to judge the wisdom of the whole.
God, he claims, acts by general, immutable law.
To act by particular voltions at each moment would
suggest rather limited foresight and a consequent
lack of wisdom. Because God acts through the
agency of general, fixed laws whatever occurs at
any time is in conformity to these laws even when
particular events seem to be disharmonious, de-
structive and harmful, for it is these same laws
which in time repair the harm and restore harmony.
In short, God knows what he is doing, even when
we do not.

Apparently convinced by these arguments, the
Chinese philosopher raises a final objection,
namely, that creation ex nihilo is an unintelli-
gible notion and that the clear idea of extension
shows, if anything, that matter is eternal. In reply Malebranche agrees that if creation means that
nothingness is the subject out of which beings are
produced, then this would certainly involve a contradiction, since the created would both be and
not be simultaneously. But such an interpretation
of the notion of creation ex nihilo involves a
fundamental misunderstanding. All being comes
from being. God is eternal, infinite and omnipotent. The models of the created universe are
eternally positioned in the essence of God. He
sees creation in himself. The nothingness of the
creature is succeeded by the being of the creature
willed into existence by God who consults his own
being. No contradiction, therefore, is involved
in this understanding of creation.

The remainder of the dialogue, like the end of
Malebranche's life as a philosopher, is taken up
with an extended discussion of the distinction between created extension and intelligible extension
an obvious final attempt to differentiate his own
position from that of "le misérable Spinoza."

## Note on the Translation

The French text on which this translation is
used is that of André Robinet, established upon
the edition of 1708.  That edition, originally
published by Michel David (Paris), was the text
referred by Malebranche.[43]  The text prepared
by Robinet forms Volume XV of the Oeuvres complètes de Malebranche, and was published in 1958
by J. Vrin of Paris as part of the series Biblio-
thètique de Textes Philosophiques directed by
Henri Gouhier.  Robinet's edition of this text
is the most thorough and accurate available and
is, indeed, the definitive text of this work.

As noted earlier, manuscript copies of the
Entretien d'un Philosophe chrétien et d'un Philosophe chinois, sur l'existence et la nature de
Dieu circulated during the latter half of 1707.
Only after the Mémoires de Trévoux published the
text in its entirety (with the exception of the
Advice to the Reader") did Malebranche seek to
publish his text, and then only with the "Advice
to the Reader."  His intention, of course, was to
reply point by point to the Jesuit criticisms
levelled at him.  This was done in 1708.

Other editions of this work appeared in 1730
and 1736.[44]  The present translation marks the
first in English and is a faithful rendering of
Robinet's excellent critical text, with the exception of a small portion of the "Advice to the
Reader" in which Malebranche cites several Jesuit
authorities for his opinion that Chinese sages
were in fact atheists.  Among those cited are
Matthew Ricci, Nicolo Longobardi, Martin Martini,
Alvares Semedo, and Claude de Visdelou, among
several others.  Also omitted is the "Privilege du
Roy."

NOTES

The most prominent European sources are: Pang
(Ching-Ien), L'idée de Dieu chez Malebranche et
l'idée de Li chez Tchou Hi, suivies de Du Li et
du K'i, traduction annotée du Livre XLIX des
oeuvres complètes de Tchou Hi, Paris, J. Vrin,
1942; Henri Maspero, La Chine antique, Histoire
du monde, tome IV, Paris, de Boccard, 1927. An
excellent translation of this work has made its
appearance recently entitled: China in Antiquity,
translated by Frank A. Kierman, University of
Massachussetts Press, 1979.  See also: P. Masson-
Oursel, La Philosophie comparée, Paris, Alcan,
1931; M. Granet, La pensée chinoise, Evolution de
l'humanité, tome XXV bis, Paris, 1934; J.J.L.
Duyvendak, Etudes de Philosophie chinoise, Révue
Philosophique, Nov.-Dec., 1930; pp. 372-417.  In
English one may consult with profit: Joseph Need-
ham, Science and Civilization in China, Vol. 2:
History of Scientific Thought, Cambridge, Cam-
bridge University Press, 1956; David E. Mungello,
Leibniz and Confucianism: The Search for Accord,
Honolulu, University Press of Hawaii, 1978.

Yves Marie André, La vie de Malebranche (extract
contained in Oeuvres complètes de Malebranche,
tome XV: Entretien d'un Philosophe chrétien et
d'un Philosophe chinois sur l'existence et la
nature de Dieu, par André Robinet, Paris, Vrin,
1958, pp. vii-ix).

The main documents concerning the "Rites Affair"
are listed in the Robinet edition of this dialogue,
pp. xxviii-xxxiv.  For more detailed discussion
see: Kenneth Scott Latourette, A History of
Christian Missions in China, New York, Russell
and Russell, (1929) 1967 (especially chapters VII
and VIII).  Also: Charles W. Allan, Jesuits at
the Court of Peking, Shangai, Kelly and Walsh,
1975.

Malebranche, Oeuvres complètes, XV, xvii.

[5] Franz R. Merkel, _G.W. Leibniz und die China-Mission_, Leipzig, 1920, pp. 100-102. See also: G.W. Leibniz, _Discourse on the Natural Theology of the Chinese_ (Society for Asian and Comparative Philosophy, Monograph No. 4), trans. and ed. with introduction and commentaries by Henry Rosemont and Daniel J. Cook, Honolulu, University Press of Hawaii, 1978.

[6] Malebranche, _Recherche de la vérité, ou l'on traite de la nature de l'esprit de l'homme, et de l'usage qu'il doit faire pour éviter l'erreur des sciences_ (Oeuvres complètes, 3 vols.), Introduction et texte etabli par Genevieve Rodis-Lewis, Paris, Vrin, 1962; I, 1. Referred to henceforth as _Recherche de la vérité_.

[7] Ibid., I, III.

[8] Ibid., III, I, I.

[9] Beatrice K. Rome (_The Philosophy of Malebranche_, Chicago, Henry Regnery Company, 1963, p. 57) sees the effort of the _Recherche de la vérité_ as a mere purification of the mind, a preliminary negative task to rid the mind of error. Similar stands are taken by Martial Gueroult, _Malebranche: La Vision en Dieu_, Paris, Aubier, 1955, Ch. IV and V, and by Henri Gouhier, _La philosophie de Malebranche et son expérience religieuse_ (Deuxième édition), Paris, Vrin, 1948, pp. 223-224.

[10] _Recherche de la vérité_, I, XIV; III, II, IV.

[11] Ibid., III, II, IV.

[12] Ibid., III, II, V. Malebranche appeals here to St. Thomas Aquinas, _Summa Theologiae_, I, 14, 6.

[13] _Recherche de la vérité_, Preface.

[14] Ibid., III, II, VI.

[15] Idem.

[16] Antoine Arnauld, _Livre de vraies et des fausses idées_ (Oeuvres de Messire Antoine Arnauld, Docteur de la Maison et Societé de Sorbonne, Paris-Lausanne, Sigismond d'Arnay et Compagnie, 1780; XXXVIII, 259), Ch. XV.

[17]Malebranche, Réponse au livre de M. Arnauld:
Des vraies et des fausses idées (Oeuvres philosophiques d'Antoine Arnauld, édité par Jules
Simon; Paris, Charpentier, 1843), XV, 1-4. See
also: Recueil de toutes les réponses du P. Malebranche à M. Arnauld (4 volumes), Paris, David,
1709, I, 173-177. Boileau is said to have ex-
claimed: "My dear sir, whom do you expect to
understand you, if M. Arnauld does not?"

[18]Arnauld, Des vraies et des fausses idées,
Ch. XV (Oeuvres, XXXVIII, 247-259.

[19]Arnauld, Défense de M. Arnauld (Oeuvres, XXXVIII,
401, 538).

[20]Malebranche, Méditations chrétiennes et métaphysiques, IX (Oeuvres complètes de Malebranche,
X, 101), édité par Henri Gouhier, Paris, Vrin,
1959.

[21]Malebranche, Première lettre contre la défense
de M. Arnauld (Recueil, I, 326). Gouhier (La
philosophie de Malebranche et son expérience
religieuse, p. 372) claims that from the Méditations chrétiennes to the Entretien d'un philosophe chrétien et d'un philosophe Chinois the
work of Malebranche is "une protestation contre
le spinozisme."

[22]Malebranche, Meditations chrétiennes et métaphysiques, IX (Oeuvres complètes de Malebranche,
X, 95-97).

[23]Ibid., IX (p. 98).

[24]Ibid., IX (pp. 99-101).

[25]Benedict Spinoza, Ethics, I Definitions III-V
(The Chief Works of Benedict Spinoza, Trans. by
R.H.M. Elwes; New York, Dover, 1955, II, 45).

[26]Ibid., I, Prop. XII-XIII (Elwes edition, II, 54).

[27]Ibid., I, Prop. V (Elwes edition, II, 47). See
also Prop. XIV (Elwes edition, II, 54-55).

[28]Ibid., I, Prop. XIX, XXI (Elwes edition, II,
62-65).

[29]Ibid., I, XV, Note (Elwes edition, II, 58).

[30] Victor Delbos, Etude de la philosophie de Malebranche, Paris, Bloud et Gay, 1924, p. 189.

[31] Malebranche, Lettre à Mairan, 29 sept. 1713 (Corréspondance inédité de Malebranche avec J.J. Dortous de Mairan. Edition nouvelle precedée d'une Introduction sur "Malebranche et le Spinozisme" par Joseph Moreau. Paris, Vrin, 1947, p. 105). Gouhier (La philosophie de Malebranche et son expérience religieuse. p. 373) suggests that Malebranche never read Spinoza entirely and what little of his work he did read he probably read only once and remained satisfied with that single reading.

[32] Malebranche, Entretien d'un Philosophe chrétien et d'un Philosophe chinois, p. 34; Entretiens sur la métaphysique et sur la religion, VIII (Edition par Armand Cuvillier. Paris, Vrin, 1961, I, 243-245); Entretiens sur la mort, II (contained in Cuvillier's edition of the Entretiens sur la métaphysique et sur la religion; II, 245; 248-251).

[33] Malebranche, Entretiens sur la métaphysique et sur la religion, VIII, vii (Cuvillier, I, 243); Malebranche à Dortous de Mairan, 12 juin 1714 (Moreau, pp. 168-170).

[34] Malebranche à Dortous de Mairan, 6 septembre 1714 (Moreau, p. 175).

[35] Yu-lan Fung, A History of Chinese Philosophy: Volume II: The Period of Classical Learning; Trans. by Derk Bodde, Princeton, Princeton University Press, 1953; p. 533. A good study of the philosophy of Chu-Hsi is by J. Percy Bruce, The Philosophy of Human Nature by Chu-Hsi, London, Probsthain, 1922.

[36] Yu-lan Fung, op. cit., p. 534; Wing-tsit Chan, A Source Book in Chinese Philosophy, Princeton, Princeton University Press, 1963, p. 637f.

[37] Wing-tsit Chan, op. cit., p. 638.

[38] Ibid., p. 641.

[39] Ibid., p. 639.

[40] Ibid., p. 642.

[41] Ibid., p. 645.

[42] Yu-lan Fung, op. cit., II, 560.

[43] The full title of the original publication is:
Entretien d'un Philosophe chrétien et d'un
Philosophe chinois, sur l'existence et la nature
de Dieu. Par l'Auteur de la Recherche de la vérité. A Paris, Chez Michel David, Quay des Augus-
tins, à la Providence. M.DCC.VIII. Avec Approbation et Privilege du Roy. (Pp. 1-73 in-12).

[44] In 1837 De Genoude and de Lourdoueix presented
an edition of the Entretien without the "Advice
to the Reader" in Volume II (pp. 365-376) of the
Oeuvres complètes de Malebranche, Paris, Sapia,
1837. Jules Simon likewise published the Entretien without the "Advice" in Volume I (pp.473-
500) of the Oeuvres de Malebranche, Paris, Charpentier, Nouvelle edition, 1842. Later editions
by Simon appeared in 1853-9 and in 1877. Finally,
A. LeMoine in 1936 edited and published the complete text (Paris, J. Vrin) accompanied by an
exposition of the work and philosophy of Malebranche.

BIBLIOGRAPHY

lan, Charles W. Jesuits at the Court of Peking.
    Shanghai: Kelly and Walsh, Limited, 1975.

nauld, Antoine. Oeuvres philosophiques d'An-
    toine Arnauld. Edité par Jules Simon. Paris:
    Charpentier, 1843.

____ Oeuvres de Messire Antoine Arnauld, Docteur
    de la Maison et Societé de Sorbonne. 42 vol-
    umes. Paris-Lausanne: Sigismond d'Arnay et
    Compagnie, 1780.

uce, J. P. The Philosophy of Human Nature by
    Chu-Hsi. London: Probsthain, 1922.

an, Wing-tsit. A Source Book in Chinese Phil-
    osophy. Princeton: Princeton University Press,
    1963.

lbos, Victor. Etude de la philosophie de Male-
    branche. Paris: Bloud et Gay, 1924.

yvendak, J.J.L. "Etudes de philosophie chinoise,"
    Révue Philosophique: Nov.- Dec., 1930, pp.372-
    417.

ng, Yu-lan. A History of Chinese Philosophy.
    Translated by Derk Bodde. 3 volumes. Prince-
    ton: Princeton University Press, 1953.

uhier, Henri. La Vocation de Malebranche.Paris:
    Vrin, 1926.

____ La philosophie de Malebranche et son expéri-
    ence religieuse. Duxième édition. Paris: Vrin,
    1948.

anet, M. La pensée chinoise, Evolution de
    l'humanité. Paris, 1934.

Gueroult, Martial. Malebranche. I: La Vision en Dieu. Paris: Aubier, 1955. II-III: Les cinq abimes de la Providence. Paris: Aubier, 1959.

Latourette, Kenneth Scott. A History of Christian Missions in China. New York: Russell and Russell, (1929) 1967.

Leibniz, Wilhelm G. Discourse on the Natural Theology of the Chinese. Society for Asian and Comparative Philosophy, Monograph No. 4. Translated and edited with introduction and commentaries by Henry Rosemont and Daniel J. Cook. Honolulu: University Press of Hawaii, 1978.

Malebranche, Nicolas. Oeuvres complètes de Malebranche. Edité par André Robinet. 20 volumes. Paris: Vrin, 1958-1965.

_____ Recueil de toutes les réponses du P. Malebranche à M. Arnauld. 4 volumes. Paris: David, 1709.

Maspero, Henri. La Chine antique. Histoire du monde, tome IV. Paris: de Boccard, 1927. China in Antiquity. Translated by Frank A. Kierman, Jr. University of Massachussetts Press, 1979.

Masson-Oursel, P. La Philosophie comparée. Paris: Alcan, 1931.

Merkel, Franz R. G.W. Leibniz und die China Mission. Leipzig, 1920.

Mungello, David E. Leibniz and Confucianism: The Search for Accord. Honolulu: University Press of Hawaii, 1978.

Needham, Joseph. Science and Civilization in China Volume 2: History of Scientific Thought. Cambridge: Cambridge University Press, 1956.

Pang, Ching-Ien. L'idée de Dieu chez Malebranche et l'idée de Li chez Tchou Hi, suivies de Du

Li et du K'i. Traduction annotée du Livre XLIX des oeuvres complètes de Tchou Hi.  Paris: Vrin, 1942.

obinet, Andre.  "Introduction," Entretien d'un Philosophe chrétien et d'un Philosophe chinois, sur l'existence et la nature de Dieu (Oeuvres complètes de Malebranche, tome XV. Paris: Vrin, 1958; pp. I-XXXIV.

ome, Beatrice K. The Philosophy of Malebranche. Chicago: Henry Regnery Company, 1963.

pinoza, Benedict.  The Chief Works of Benedict Spinoza. Translated by R.H.M. Elwes. New York: Dover, 1955.  Two volumes.

# DIALOGUE BETWEEN A CHRISTIAN PHILOSOPHER AND A CHINESE PHILOSOPHER ON THE EXISTENCE AND NATURE OF GOD

By

Nicolas Malebranche

## ADVICE TO THE READER

A very respectable person, deserving of credit if ever there was one, has assured me that through the exchange he has had with Chinese scholars he has found that their opinions on divinity were such that I should undertake to expose them. He has begged me many times to refute them, but in a manner that makes use of truths they might accept in order to rectify the false idea they have of the nature of God. I have been convinced of a special obligation to obey him, hoping that perhaps my reasons might serve the missionaries who work toward the conversion of these people. I do not know whether, in order to justify my obedience, I should add that the person of whom I speak has assured me that the Chinese would strongly agree with my positions and that in a letter from a Jesuit Father from China to his confreres in France I have read the sense of these words: Do not send us any of your savants in philosophy, but those who know mathematics and the works of Father Malebranche. Nevertheless, it is neither on account of the command of this person that I speak nor on account of my own concerns that the dialogue has been published. The approval was obtained without even being sought by me. I did not regard this booklet as a present worthy of being offered to the public. I avow, however, that I yielded to a desire of my friends that it be published, and that for two reasons: the first, because it was pointed out to me that I demonstrated in it some truths of extreme consequence, and that it might serve to refute irreligion. Those who read it with care will judge of what is in it. The second reason is that the manuscript copies having been scattered throughout the world, there circulated a rumor that I wrote against the Jesuit fathers. I believed that with the appearance of my work this unfounded rumor would be dispelled.

Here, therefore, are what I have been informed are the errors of the Chinese philosophers and

what I have intended to combat in my writing. Had
I had it published myself, I would have exposed
these errors immediately in a preface. That would
appear necessary to prepare the mind for the reading of this brief work.

Chinese scholars, at least those with whom the
person who has instructed me about their positions
has conversed, believe:
1) that there are only two kinds of beings, namely, the Li, or Supreme Reason, Law, Wisdom,
   Justice, and matter;
2) that the Li and matter are eternal beings;
3) that the Li does not subsist in itself and independently of matter. Apparently, they regard
   it as a form or quality diffused throughout
   matter;
4) that the Li is neither wise nor intelligent, although it is supreme wisdom and intelligence;
5) that the Li is not free and that it acts only
   by the necessity of its nature, without knowing
   or willing anything of what it does;
6) that it renders intelligent, wise and just the
   parts of matter disposed to receive intelligence,
   wisdom and justice. For according to these
   scholars, the mind of man is only purified matter or matter disposed to be informed by the Li,
   and thereby rendered intelligent or capable of
   thought. It is apparently because of that that
   they agree that the Li is the light which enlightens all men and that it is in it that we
   see all things.

The above are in general the errors and paradoxes which I have had in mind in my writing and which
a friend has desired that I should refute.

Since it is four or five months that it has been
published, it has come to the attention of the
journalists of Trevoux. Someone among them has
manifestly read it a little too precipitously and
with bias and prepared a critique of it. I shall
proceed to report it in its entirety so that by a
comparison of the pieces in hand one might judge

solidly, not the capacity of the author, who no doubt could do better, but his fairness toward me. For he tries, it seems, to give birth to certain assumptions about which it is not permitted me to be silent; not solely on account of the quality of the author but also on account of the multiplicity of copies of their journals which speak and will speak in the future to all who would read them.

Here is the critique, drawn from the Mémoires de Trévoux of 1708.

## ARTICLE LXXXIX

"Dialogue Between a Christian Philosopher and a Chinese Philosopher on the Existence and Nature of God, etc.

The author of the Recherche de la vérité and of this dialogue imputes atheism to a Chinese philosopher without ceremony, while he, under the name of a Christian philosopher, attempts to convince him by special arguments. Perhaps not every Chinese philosopher or every Christian philosopher agrees with what is here said by the one or the other. So much is at least certain with regard to the Emperor of China, who is as far removed from atheism as he is a sage in the philosophy of his nation."

REMARK. The words "he imputes atheism to a Chinese philosopher without ceremony" mean to imply that in so doing I am not justified. So, since there is not a single Chinese who subscribes to atheism and who, without harming the truth, could serve me as an interlocutor in order to refute impiety, there is no satisfying the delicacy of the author but to change Chinese to Japanese or Siamese, or rather, to French; for it happens that the system of the impious Spinoza wreaks great havoc here; and it seems to me that there are many correspondences between the impieties of Spinoza and those of the Chinese philosopher.

The change of name would not change anything in what is essential to my writing. I implore the author not to place in my mouth anything save the proofs that I adduce against the errors some have desired that I refute and to leave me, instead, the liberty to believe the facts guaranteed me by a person about whom I have no doubt concerning his probity and sincerity.

For the rest, I do not place atheism in the mouth of the Chinese, unless one means by atheism the refusal to recognize the existence of the true God, of being infinitely perfect in every manner. If the learned Chinese adore the material heaven, or even the Lord of Heaven, and consider this Lord as one being among many, a being limited and finite in his essence, such as a powerful king similar, for example, to the Jupiter of the pagans, the conqueror of the Giants and of the Titans, which they would call the God of Heaven, they are as much idolators as they would be if they adored Pluto, the Lord of Hell, or Beelzebub, the God of insects. I wish to believe on the word of the author that the Emperor of China recognizes and adores the true God, the infinitely perfect being, in a word, He Who Is, for it is the absolute name that God gives to himself. I desire likewise with all my heart that the Jesuit fathers obtain from him a public declaration on this matter; for apparently he has confided in them these fine sentiments, since we have been told here "that it is certain that he is very far removed from atheism."

THE AUTHOR. "Before coming to the demonstration of the existence of God, it is necessary to establish the notion, and thus he says: 'Our God is He Who Is, infinitely perfect being, Being. This King of Heaven whom you regard as our God is only a kind of being, a particular being, a finite being. Our God is being without restriction or limitation. He even includes within himself, in a manner incomprehensible to every finite mind, whatever true reality there is in all beings, both

48

created and possible.

REMARK. This text is taken from the third page of my work. But in the line I have noted by an asterisk he has omitted these words, "all the perfections." It is necessary to read the third and fourth page and even the seventeenth in order to better judge of what follows.

THE AUTHOR. "It falls to the Chinese now to warn all the missionaries not to use any longer the word Tien-chu, that is to say, Lord of Heaven, to signify God. But if he is converted and reads the Sacred Scriptures, he would be very astonished to find therein on each page that God is the Lord and the King of Heaven and of earth, and above all that God is a kind of being, a particular being, absolutely distinguished from all others, and infinitely elevated above all others, and of which consequently he does not include at all in himself the reality, although he contains all their perfections eminently. Just as every created thing participates after its manner in the perfections of God and not in his reality, so likewise God, after his manner, includes the perfections which he has conferred and not the reality of his work. But it is necessary to believe that the word reality is here referred to that of perfections, as there is reason to infer from what the author says, that created beings are not parts of God but infinitely imperfect imitations of his essence alone. In giving instructions it would be appropriate to avoid terms which have a misleading meaning; above all at a time when the impious system of Spinoza wreaks secret havoc."

REMARK. Since I assume that the reader has read with attention the third and fourth page and also the seventeenth, from which the author quotes some words, I believe that I do not have great need to respond, except to present some reflections on this discourse of the author.

I do not see why, concerning what I have said

49

in the transcribed line that the Christian God is
He Who Is, infinitely perfect being, and the rest,
I do not see why, I say, the author concludes from
it "that it falls to the Chinese to warn all the
missionaries not to use any longer the word Tien-
chu, Lord of Heaven, to signify God." I confess
that Lord of Heaven, and even Heaven, are terms of
which one may make use in speaking of God, because they can awaken in the mind the true notion
of God, with regard to those who already recognize
it. When the Christians say, for example, that it
is from Heaven that one must seek peace, one sees
easily that by Heaven is intended the true God.
But it is on account of this that one assumes that
they understand it and do not adore anything else.
Lord of Heaven is only a name of quality, a relative name. But He Who Is, or, infinitely perfect
being, is an absolute name which expresses the
essence of the true God and which can belong only
to him. God can without doubt make an angel Lord
of Heaven, and grant him the power to regulate the
movement of the stars; but such a Lord of Heaven
would not be the God of the Christians. "If therefore the Chinese is converted," but is truly converted, "and if he reads the Scriptures," he would
not at all be "surprised to find," if he looks "on
each page," that God is the Lord and King of Heav-
en. For he would know that he is actual and that
he does not resemble Jupiter whom the pagans call
Lord of Heaven. He would not even be surprised to
learn that the Sacred Scriptures give to God arms
and hands, eyes and ears, because having grasped
in the same scripture that the true God is He Who
Is, infinitely perfect being, infinitely good, wise,
just, powerful and the rest, he would comprehend
that if such expressions frequently humanize the
Divinity it is only because they accomodate themselves to the weakness of men.

Further, I do not perceive on what ground the
author insinuates here and further down that my
opinion could be that God is not a kind of being
or "a particular being distinguished from all
others," but one composed of all the parts of the

verse, which is the impiety of Spinoza; and
t, above all, after having read the seventeenth
e from which he cites these words, in which
e I precisely note in what sense one must say
t God is and is not a kind of being, or a par-
ular being. I beg the reader to read the sev-
eenth page with some attention. I do not un-
stand how the author fails to understand that
n I say that God is not a kind of being or a
d of good, when I do not even add **what** I have
ays added, a limited being, a finite good, I
n by that that God is Being or the good in
ch all other beings participate as being but
erfect and finite imitations of his essence.
id plura et plura," says St. Augustine,* "bon-
hoc et bonum illud? Tolle hoc et illud, et
e ipsum bonum, si potes, ita Deum videbis; non
o bono bonum, sed bonum omnis boni." But, adds
author, "There is reason to infer that the
d reality is here used for that of perfection."
re was not only <u>reason</u>, but there was <u>necessity</u>
believe it, if he had quoted my text exactly
if he had not suppressed the words "all the
fections," which without the conjunctive and
itive particle AND are on the third page before
l there is of true reality." I did not even
these last, which in accordance with the ad-
e that the author gives me, I perhaps feared
much "that one not take the words in the mis-
ding sense."

THE AUTHOR. "Notice, however, the demonstra-
n. 'To think nothing and not to think, to per-
ve nothing and not to perceive is the same
ng. Therefore, whatever the mind perceives
ediately and directly is something, or exists...
I think the infinite, I perceive immediately
directly the infinite. Therefore, it is.
if it were not I would perceive nothing. Hence.
the very same moment I would perceive and not

<u>Trinitate</u>, Lib. 8, cap. 3.

51

perceive anything, which is a manifest contradiction.' If it is only an infinite which includes in itself the reality of an infinity of
things that our mind conceives, it does not do
enough to advance the existence of God. It is
necessary to say, therefore, that we conceive
the infinite in all perfections, and consequently
the infinite in existence, and by this same infinity distinguished from all others. After this
demonstration is grounded uniquely on the notion
we have of God, one should not attend at all to
what the author adds: 'While the perception by
which this idea touches us is the lightest of all,
the more light as it is the more vast, and consequently infinitely light because it is infinite.
For after all what can be the solidity of an argument established on a perception the most light of
all, and infinitely light?"

RESPONSE. One of the greatest obstacles which
impedes men from recognizing the reality of abstract ideas which do not modify the mind at all
by sensible perceptions is that they ordinarily
judge the reality of ideas only by the sensibility
of the perceptions by which they touch their mind.
It is for this reason that I have the Chinese say
that even though he is reduced to having nothing
to reply to my arguments, he is not convinced; because it seems to him always that when he thinks
of the infinite he thinks of nothing. I try to have
him realize the extravagance of his bias on the
eleventh page and in the succeeding ones. I reveal the cause to him and try to get him to understand this truth: That he must not judge of the
reality of ideas, not even of their efficacy, on
the basis of the lesser or greater liveliness of
the perceptions by which they touch us, but by the
greater or lesser reality that the mind discovers
in them. For the same idea can not only affect us
successively with a great number of entirely different perceptions, but even, as I prove by experience, by several different ones at the same
time. And that thus, although the infinite touches us in this life by a very light perception, it

52

pearing one thinks nothing in thinking it, it is
ntrary to reason to imagine that it has less re-
ity than the finite by reason of the fact that
e idea of the finite touches us with interesting
d lively perceptions. Assuming that one has read
th sufficient attention the lines of the dia-
gue which I have noted, one can judge the rest
the text I have quoted. For me it seems that
e author wished to amuse his reader at my ex-
nse, or else he does not comprehend anything of
at he criticizes. This seems certain from the
xt that I have quoted, and even the author seems
 sincerely agree.

THE AUTHOR. "Passing on to the manner by which
 know, he distinguishes between idea and under-
anding. 'The former is the immediate object of
e latter and is in itself the essence of God
ich can, by touching me by his efficacious re-
ities (for there is nothing in God of impotence),
at is, in touching me by his essence insofar as
 is participable by all beings, reveal to me or
present to me all beings. It is thus,' he says,
hat God makes us see all things in him without
king himself seen.' Suppose, he adds, in order
 explain his thought, that the surface of this
ll were capable of acting on your mind and to
ke itself seen by it. It is clear that it could
ke you see all the curved and straight lines and
l sorts of figures without your seeing the surf-
e itself. For if the surface should touch you
ly insofar as it is a line and the remainder of
is surface did not touch you at all and became
rfectly transparent, you would see the line with-
t seeing the surface, although you would not see
e line except on the surface."

REMARK. It would have been appropriate, it
ems, if the author had taken the pain to quote
at follows: "and by the action of the surface
 your mind, because in effect this surface in-
udes the reality of all sorts of lines. Thus,
d, infinitely perfect being and including
inently in himself all there is of reality or

53

perfection in all beings, can represent them to us by touching us with his essence, not understood absolutely, but insofar as it is relative to these beings, since his infinite essence includes all there is of true reality in all finite beings. Thus God alone acts immediately on our souls. He alone is our life, our light, our wisdom, etc."

THE AUTHOR. "But it seems that the surface, having become transparent, would no longer touch the mind and that the line would then be seen in itself."

REMARK. It is precisely such that I mean to conclude from my gross comparison. One would then see the line without seeing the surface. One can therefore see immediately or in themselves the ideas of beings which are in God without seeing God himself. One can see his essence insofar as it is relative to created and possible beings without seeing his essence taken absolutely. It is uniquely this which I wanted to make clear, and it is this which consequently destroys what the author tells us.

THE AUTHOR. "But let us assume further: (1) that God touches our mind by his essence; (2) that his essence contains in itself the reality of all beings, even if, according to the author, it has its proper reality, not being at all a particular being; (3) that these realities, whatever they may be, are in themselves efficacious. It seems to follow from this that the efficacious essence and efficacious realities together touch our mind, may themselves seen together, and cause an uninterrupted perception by which God is seen in himself or in his essence; and all things are seen in God or in the essence of God."

REMARK. I invite the reader to try to understand this statement and above all to compare it with that which preceded, so that by doing so he may feel the embarrassment I find myself in of trying to respond with some precision to a man who

riticizes what seems to me he does not understand.
ll I can do is repeat that I believe* that God
ouches our mind by his essence; I add, immedi-
tely and directly "NULLA interposita creatura,"
s St. Augustine says, but not according to what
his Divine essence is in itself or taken ab-
olutely, but relatively to his creatures, that
s, as St. Thomas explains it in I, Q. 15, a. 2,
nsofar as it includes ideas. This is what I be-
ieve I have clearly demonstrated in several of my
orks and even at some length in my last response
o a third posthumous letter by M. Arnauld. I
ite in fact this last response rather than the
thers which he may find hard to locate in order
o excite the curiosity of the author to read it
nd thereby place him in a position to judge my
entiment from knowledge of the matter. For the
est I believe it is necessary to say that it is
hese offensive words, joined to those which I have
eported and to which I have already responded:
Even if, according to the author, the divine
ssence has its proper reality, God is not at all
 particular being," which have placed me in the
npleasant and disagreeable position of having to
espond and to demand of the author before the
hole world how, after having read my dialogue and,
bove all, the seventeenth page from which he even
uotes some words, he could form, and what is
orse,publish so cruel a conjecture. I pray God
o pardon his fault and beg the author to make
eparation by having printed in the same Mémoires
e Trevoux my response to his criticism, so that
he one and the other may have the same readers;
r at least that he make reparation by means of
rayers so that Jesus Christ grants me the neces-
ary assistance to control the agitation of my
eart on the precept that he has given us to love
hose who have offended us.

THE AUTHOR. "A wise reader who does not find
n himself such insights that are more extensive

See the Preface of the Entretiens sur la Métaphysique et sur la Religion.

55

than that of beatitude reduces himself to saying
to himself that he is not always bright enough to
understand the author entirely. He would avow
that he is not initiated in such mysteries as:
'idea distinguished from understanding and which
is the essence of God, of realities of things in
God, and concerning the essence of God which touches the mind of man.' But perhaps he would recall
on such an occasion a quotation from Cicero concerning the nature of gods: 'Ego enim scire te
ista melius quam me, non fateor tantum, sed fa-
cile patior. Cum quidem dicta sunt: quid est;
quod Velleius possit, Cotta non possit.'"

REMARK. At times "a wise reader," who flatters
himself a bit too much, can, to console himself
concerning the reading he does not understand well,
say to himself "he is not always bright enough to
understand the author entirely." But apparently
this wise reader does not entertain this judgment
of his. He avows simply and modestly that he does
not understand the position of the author without
failing to avail himself of such scornful expressions as: "I am not initiated in these mysteries,
idea is distinguished from understanding and is the
essence of God, and the like." For it seems to me
not only is it to decide that the idea and the
consciousness or the perception one has of it are
only the same thing, but even more to treat the
contrary position as extravagant and ridiculous for
nothing [sic] worse. However, let the author permit
me to show him that to maintain "that ideas are
not distinguished from our perceptions" is, if I
am not mistaken, to establish invincibly Pyrrhon-
ism in the sciences and Libertinism in morals. It
is to maintain what is without doubt most foreign
to the thinking of the author. It is, I say, indirectly  but by consequences which seem to me
evident and necessary to maintain that there are
no eternal, immutable, necessary truths common to
all minds, or even similar laws, for the one follows from the other. Here are some proofs.

It is evident that truths are only relations

hich exist between ideas. Two and two make four,
nd two and two do not make five are truths only
ecause there is a relation of equality between
wo and two and four, and of inequality between
wo and two and five, that is, two and two is the
ame thing as four and two and two is less than
ive. If therefore the numbering numbers that St.
ugustine calls "divine and eternal" and which are
he ideas by which we count the things numbered are
ot "distinguished from the fleeting perceptions"
f our mind, certainly the truths of numbers would
ot be eternal and immutable, for our perceptions
r our understandings would not be before us and
here could be no different relations between
othings.

It is usual to admit this principle: That one
an affirm of a thing what one clearly conceives
o be included in the idea one has of it. But if
he idea one has is not distinguished from the per-
eption, or from the modification of the mind which
erceives it, this principle is not certain. For
urely God has not created beings based on our
leeting perceptions, but on eternal ideas: which
deas we perceive when they touch us and by them
he beings which are necessarily conformed to them.
 omit many other reasons which could also be used.
 say only that, assuming that ideas are not dis-
inguished from our perceptions, whoever perceives
hat the three angles of a triangle are equal to
wo right angles can be very sure that what he
erceives he perceives, or that that seems so to
im, which the Pyrrhonians would agree with. But
t is not right to be sure that it is so and that
ll men, all intelligences and God himself see it
s he does and that it is an immutable, necessary,
ternal truth; for surely his own perception is
ot such. If therefore there are eternal and im-
utable truths, ideas are eternal and immutable;
nd as such it is evident that they cannot be
ound save in the eternal and immutable essence
f Divinity itself.

The author must not, therefore, (I add nothing) so much as admit of the true and the false, of the just and the unjust as necessarily so, of eternal, necessary, immutable truths and eternal laws common to all minds, since he confuses ideas with states of consciousness or perceptions of the soul. It is not fitting to God that I form of him such a conjecture, although it would be better founded than the one I have just complained about. I have no doubt at all about the contrary. The author, I say, should not declare with a mocking air that "he is not initiated into these mysteries of the idea distinguished from consciousness" and the rest, nor add his passage from Cicero. For after all, the question he raises is serious and of extreme consequence. Since I have read more St. Augustine than Cicero, I may be permitted to quote this brief statement which I have read in his first book <u>Against the Academicians</u>: "Quoeso ut ratio proeveniat risum tuum: nihil enim est foedius risu irrisione dignissimo." At a time when the errors of the English authors Hobbes, Locke and others are everywhere and <u>wreak very great havoc</u>, too great to remain secret, it is necessary not to mock this principle: that ideas are different from the perceptions we have of them; that they are eternal and immutable, and our perceptions are fleeting. For without this principle which I believe I have clearly demonstrated in my responses to M. Arnauld and others, I do not see that one could by reason correct the course of their very dangerous errors.

To judge what follows one must of necessity read carefully in the dialogue from page 57 to 66,* and should one find some obscurity which I hope will not happen, one can turn to the <u>Entretiens sur la métaphysique et sur la religion</u>, where I treat more fully of divine Providence.

THE AUTHOR. "To justify Providence which allows

*See pages 93-98. - Tr.

arvests to be ravaged and makes us suffer so many
ccidents, this author says that God loves his
isdom more than his work, which is certainly true.
e has only to explain it well. Now Divine wisdom
as dictated that he employ some very simple
rinciples for the creation of the world and not
o interrupt its course when it leads to these in-
onveniences about which we complain.  There is
ome truth in that; but in effect would God be
erpetually making miracles in order to impede and
hange the direction of natural causes?"

  REMARK.  It is morally impossible to guess from
his statement what is my thought and very difficult
o be sure of the author's. He says that according
o my thinking "the wisdom of God has dictated that
e employ some very simple principles for the cre-
tion of the world."  I know quite well that I have
ever maintained this.  If there is some truth in
hat, as the author claims, I cannot discern it.
od, according to my way of thinking, has employed
o other <u>principle</u> for creation than an act of
is all powerful will. I judge the following words
nd not to interrupt its course," and so on,
very simple principles," and that the wisdom of
od dictated to him their employment for the "cre-
tion of the world," to mean for the author "nat-
al causes." But certainly before the creation of
e world there were none of these "natural caus-
, by which its course leads to inconveniences."
 must be, therefore, it seems to me, that he has
advertently placed the "creation" of the world
 place of the "governance" of the world.  There
uld be truth in that. For God employs secondary
uses in the governance of the world.  But his
atement, however construed, confers on my posi-
on an idea so general and confused that even
en, which is not the case, I do not agree with
ything he says in what follows, the reader would
t see how my position, which he does not under-
and at all, would be solidly refuted.

  Since I myself feel that I am boring my reader,
will only continue to the end of the author's

text so that one will have it in its entirety, without scrupulously examining its meaning. I shall only add some responses between parentheses.

THE AUTHOR. "But if one bears in mind that principles are called simple or composed only in relation to what must result from them, one could easily understand that it would have been from the same wisdom to put other principles in operation in order to form another world, and more principles for a more perfect world. Just as it is the same skill for an architect to employ more and richer materials for a larger and more magnificent building, or just as it is the same skill for a watchmaker to use a greater number of wheels for the striking parts, the alarm clock, the minutes, and the repeater. (I agree, and I even said not the words but the sense of all of this in the dialogue, page 60 and 62,[*] and more fully elsewhere, as in my last response to M. Arnauld, page 265 and 271, and in the first volume of the Entretiens sur la Métaphysique, page 268 on Since therefore the wisdom of God did not demand that he should create the world as it is or more perfectly, it is necessary to arrive at what common sense and religion have led the Fathers to say when they had to respond to the Epicureans and the Manichaeans, enemies of Providence; that the world with its supposed defects bears in its beauty and its constant order the traits of an infinite wisdom and a power as infinite, and that the discomforts we would like not to feel serve to test the good and punish the wicked to the end that God knows how to draw an even greater good from what appears to us to be an evil. (I agree again with everything here, justly interpreted. Common sense and religion have made me say and write it often. I say justly interpreted, for I do not agree that there is no evil but only the appearance of it. I believe there is evil, that God permits it, and that he draws good from it. I als

[*]See pages 95-96. - Tr.

believe that there are in the world not only supposed defects, but real defects which occur, as
one says in school, ob defectum causarum secund-
arum.  But all this is only tangential.  I respond to the objection of the Chinese.  It would
be necessary to examine whether my response is
solid or contrary "to common sense and to religion."  I do not see that "common sense" demanded
that I should derive the origin of evil from
original sin in responding to the Chinese, whom
I assumed never to have spoken about this sin.
To say to him also that our actual sins are the
cause of our evils would have been to involve
myself in explaining to him why then the greatest
sinners are in this world not the most miserable,
which would have placed me in the position of
leaving aside my subject and telling him many
truths that Christians know but of which he had
no understanding or which he would have perhaps
regarded as wasted.  In the end, one can not and
one should not always say everything; and I have
not supposed that there could not be other responses than mine to prove to the Chinese that the "Li
is not intelligent, since he allows blindness in
infants with two eyes," and so on.)  The author
continues. "For the rest the Chinese philosopher,
less by reason of the genius of his nation than
because of his astonishment at so many subtleties,
ceases to render himself contentious.  He thus
proceeds to explain his system: 'We accept only
matter and Li, that supreme truth, wisdom, and
justice which subsists eternally in matter, which
forms it and arranges it in this marvelous order
which we see, and which also enlightens this
portion of purified and organized matter of which
we are composed.  For it is necessarily in this
supreme truth, to which all men are united, some
more and some less, that they see the truths and
eternal laws which are the bonds of all societies.'"
(One might perhaps be led to believe by these
words of the author: "the Chinese philosopher
ceases to render himself contentious because of
his astonishment at so many subtleties," one might
be led to believe I say, that this philosopher

does not explain his system until the end of the dialogue after having heard all the subtleties that the Christian philosopher had to tell him. But one would seriously err. The Christian had not yet even opened his mouth, had not yet declared any of these subtleties to which the Chinese "because of his astonishment no longer renders himself contentious." For it is the Chinese who opens the conversation and who declares at once his system). "Whoever recognizes the necessity of such a principle has already taken a great step toward the existence of God. It remains only to disengage him from matter. But it is what the Chinese adds, that the Li is without consciousness and without wisdom, and who is for him eternally subsistent wisdom and a strange contradiction, that authorizes the Jesuit missionaries in China to maintain that the philosophy of the nation condemns atheism and teaches the existence of God, Creator and King of Heaven and Earth."

REMARK. The Chinese of the dialogue does not add that the "Li is without wisdom." He is, according to him, wisdom and the law, or justice, itself. But he does say that he is not wise, because he is better and more excellent than the wise. For according to him, wisdom which alone renders wise is worth more than the wise, and there is nothing as excellent, nothing as good as the Li or wisdom. He even believes that there is a contradiction in saying that wisdom is wise, because the form and the subject must be different. When this same Chinese says further that the Li is the "eternally subsistent truth and wisdom," he adds "in matter," because he does not believe that it can subsist in itself independently of matter. These are the errors of this Chinese that I seek to refute. I do not speak at all of others. But, says the author, these are "strange contradictions" which authorize the Jesuits and so on. Indeed, if men did not fall so often into "strange contradictions." But the religion of the pagans proves the contrary.

There are found many strange paradoxes. Father
Malebranche, or the Christian philosopher, avows
them and even reproaches the Chinese with them.
He did not believe he would shock any person by
trying to disabuse him of them and getting him
to understand how the true Li, the God of the
Christians, is wise in himself and is the wisdom
which renders wise all who are wise.  It is im-
agined that there are Christians who might read
with pleasure and with some profit the explanation
which I give from page 44 to 53 and that it might
be useful to the missionaries in China and to the
Jesuits themselves who make use of these books
for the conversion of these people.  It is the
testimony which actually renders to him his con-
science and his memory.  But, he says, "the philosophy of the Chinese nation condemns atheism and
teaches the existence of God, Creator and King of
Heaven and Earth."  I strongly doubt that, because it is permitted to me to do so, and I desire
nothing more, for that is commanded of me. But
there is a fact which I do not see or which I do
not understand at all. "Chinese philosophy condemns atheism."  Does not that of Europe condemn
it?  And does that prevent me from believing that
there are some Spinozists and keeping me from
producing a dialogue between a Christian and a
Spinozist in order to combat the strange paradoxes of this impious person?  If some persons
instructed in the truths of religion are capable
of falling into atheism, what must one think of
the Chinese who have not been enlightened, as we
have been, by the light of the Gospel?

DIALOGUE BETWEEN A CHRISTIAN PHILOSOPHER
AND A CHINESE PHILOSOPHER ON THE
EXISTENCE AND NATURE OF GOD


THE CHINESE. Who is this Lord of Heaven which
you have come from a distance to proclaim to us?
We do not recognize him at all; and we do not wish
to believe anything save insofar as evidence obliges us to believe. That is why we accept only
matter and Li, that Supreme Truth, Wisdom, and
justice which subsists eternally in matter, which
forms and arranges it in this marvelous order
which we see, and which also enlightens this portion of purified and organized matter of which we
are composed. For it is necessarily in this Supreme Truth, to which all men are united, some
more and some less, that they see the truths and
eternal laws which are the bonds of all societies.

THE CHRISTIAN. The God which we proclaim to
you is that same whose idea is imprinted in you
and in all men. But for want of attention to it,
they do not recognize at all what it is and
strangely disfigure it. That is why God, in order
for us to revive his idea, has declared to us
through his prophet, that he is He Who Is; that is
to say, the Being who contains in his essence all
there is of reality or of perfection in all beings, the Being infinite in every sense, in a
word, Being.

When we call "Lord of Heaven" the God whom we
adore, you imagine that we conceive him only as a
great and powerful emperor. Your Li, your supreme
justice, approaches infinitely closer the idea of
our God than that of this powerful emperor. Unde-
ceive yourselves regarding our doctrine. I repeat
to you, our God is He Who Is; he is infinitely
perfect being; he is Being. This King of Heaven
which you regard as our God is only a kind of being, only a particular being, only a finite being.
Our God is Being without any restriction or limi-
ation. He embraces within himself in a manner

65

incomprehensible to any finite mind, all perfections, everything that is truly real in all beings, both created and possible. He even contains within himself whatever reality or perfection there is in matter, the least and most imperfect of beings; but without its imperfections, its limitation, its nonbeing; for there is no nonbeing in Being, no limitation of any kind in the infinite. My hand is not my head, my chair, my room nor my mind or yours. The mind embraces, so to speak, an infinity of nonbeings, the nonbeings of all those things which it itself is not. But in the infinitely perfect Being there is nothing of nonbeing. Our God is everything that he is wherever he is; and he is everywhere. Do not attempt to comprehend how this is so. For you are finite, and the attributes of the infinite would not be its attributes at all if a finite mind could comprehend them. One can demonstrate that this is so; but one cannot explain how it is so. One can only prove that it must be incomprehensible and inexplicable to every finite mind.

THE CHINESE. I agree that this idea which you present to me of your God is the most excellent of all, for there is nothing greater than what is infinite in every manner. But we deny that this infinite being exists. It is a fiction, a fancy without reality.

THE CHRISTIAN. You maintain---and with reason--that there is a supreme law and a supreme truth which enlightens all men and is responsible for the wonderful order in the universe. If someone were to say to you that this supreme truth is no more than a fiction of your mind, how would you prove to him its existence? Surely, the proof of its existence is no more than a sequel to that of the infinitely perfect Being. You shall see this very shortly. But here, however, is a very simple and natural demonstration of the existence of God, and the most simple of all those which I could give you.

66

To think of nothing and not to think at all, to perceive nothing and not to perceive at all, are the same thing. Therefore, everything that the mind perceives immediately and directly is something or exists. Notice that I say immediately and directly. For I know very well, for example, that when one is asleep, and even in many experiences when one is awake, one thinks of things which do not exist. But then it is not these things which is the immediate and direct object of our mind. The immediate object of our mind, even in our dreams, is very real. For if this object were nothing, there would be no difference in our dreams; for there is no difference between nothings. Therefore, again, everything which the mind perceives immediately really exists. Now I think the infinite, I perceive immediately and directly the infinite. Therefore, it exists. For if it were not, in perceiving it I would perceive nothing; therefore I would not perceive. Thus, at the same time I would be both perceiving and not perceiving, which is a manifest contradiction.

THE CHINESE. I acknowledge that if the immediate object of your mind be the infinite, when you think of it, it would be the case necessarily that it exist. But then the immediate object of your mind is nothing else but your own mind. I mean that you do not perceive the infinite except insofar as this portion of organized and subtle matter, which you call mind, represents it to you. Hence, it does not at all follow that the infinite exists absolutely and outside of us, as we understand it.

THE CHRISTIAN. One could manifestly make the same response in regard to the Li or the Sovereign Truth which you admit through the first of your principles: but this would be to answer you only indirectly. Take care, I pray you. This portion of organized and subtle matter which you call mind is really finite. One can not therefore, in seeing it immediately, see the infinite. Certainly, where there are only two realities, one cannot perceive four. For there would be two realities which one would perceive and which nevertheless would not be at all. Now what is not cannot be perceived. To perceive nothing and not to perceive at all is the same thing. It is therefore evident that in a portion of finite matter or in a finite mind, one cannot find sufficient reality in it to see there the infinite. Be attentive to this. The idea which you have of the heavens is very vast. But do you not feel in yourself that the idea of space surpasses it infinitely? Does not this idea declare to you that despite any effort of your mind to traverse it, you will never exhaust it, because in effect it has no limits? But if your mind, your own substance, does not contain sufficient reality to discover within yourself the infinite in extension, a kind of infinite, a particular infinite, how can you see within it the infinite in the full sense of being, being infinitely perfect, in a word, Being? I could ask you how matter, as subtle as you wish to make it, can represent that which it is not? Or, how some organs, particular and subject to change, can either see or represent to themselves truths and eternal laws, immutable and common to all men; for your opinions seem to me to be untenable paradoxes?

THE CHINESE. Your reasoning seems valid, but it is not solid, for it is contrary to experience. You fail to recognize that a small canvas can represent to us vast fields or a large and magnificent palace. It is therefore not necessary that that which represents contain in itself the whole reality which it represents.

THE CHRISTIAN. A small canvas can represent to us vast fields. A simple discourse or a description of a palace can also represent it to us. But it is neither the canvas nor the discourse which is the immediate object of the mind that sees the palace or the fields. Even the material palaces we look at are not the immediate object of the mind

68

which sees them. It is the idea of the palace;
it is what touches or what actually affects the
mind that is its immediate object. It is certain
that a canvas represents fields only because it
reflects the light which, entering our eyes and
exciting our optic nerve and through it our brain,
(in the same way that the fields themselves do),
thereby stimulates some natural laws of the union of soul and body, the ideas which alone
represent truly the objects and which alone are
the immediate object of the mind. For you must
know that one does not see at all material objects
in themselves. One does not see them at all immediately and directly, because one often sees
some which do not exist at all. This is a truth
one can demonstrate in a hundred ways.

THE CHINESE. I agree. But I would say that
it is in the Li that we see all things. For it
is our light. It is the supreme truth, as well
as order and law. It is in it that I see the
heavens and perceive these infinite spaces which
are beyond the heavens which I see.

THE CHRISTIAN. Why in the Li? Return to the
beginning. To perceive nothing and not to perceive at all is the same thing. Therefore, one
cannot perceive a hundred realities where there
are only ten, for there would be ninety which,
not existing at all, would not be capable of being
perceived. Therefore, one cannot perceive in the
Li everything, if he does not contain eminently
all beings, if the Li is not the infinitely perfect being, which is the God which we adore. It
is in him that we can see the sky and these infinite spaces which we strongly feel incapable of
erasing, for in effect he embraces within himself
all reality. But nothing finite contains the
infinite. From the sole fact that we perceive
the infinite, it is necessary that it exists. All
of this is founded on this very evident and very
simple principle, that nothingness (le neant)
cannot be directly perceived, and that to perceive
nothing and not to perceive at all is the same

thing.

THE CHINESE. I acknowledge in good faith that I have nothing to reply to your demonstration of the existence of infinite Being. However, I have not been at all convinced. It always seems to me that when I think of the infinite, I think of nothing.

THE CHRISTIAN. But why nothing? When you think of a foot of extension or of matter, you are thinking of something. When you perceive a hundred or a thousand of them, assuredly what you perceive has a hundred or a thousand times more reality. Increase it to infinity and you will conceive without difficulty that whoever thinks the infinite is infinitely removed from thinking nothing, since what you will be thinking of is greater than everything you have thought of. But notice what is the case. The perception with which the infinite touches you is so feeble that you count for nothing what touches you so lightly. I shall explain myself.

When a thorn pricks you, the idea of the thorn produces in your soul a sensible perception called pain. When you look at the extension of your room, its idea produces in your soul a less lively perception called color. But when you look into the open air, the perception that these spaces, or rather that the idea of these spaces produces in you has no, or almost no, vividness. In fine, when you close your eyes, the idea of immense spaces which you then conceive does not affect you at all except by a purely intellectual perception. But I beg you, is it necessary to judge of the reality of ideas by the vividness of perceptions which they produce in us? If that is so, it would be necessary to believe that there is more of reality in the point of a thorn which pricks us, in a coal which burns us, or in their ideas, than there is in the entire universe or in its idea. It is surely necessary to judge of the reality of ideas by that which one sees s contained in them. Infants believe that air is nothing because the perception they have of it is not sensible. But philosophers know very well that there is as much matter in a cubic foot of air as there is in a cubic foot of lead. It seems, on the contrary, that ideas ought to affect us with at least as great a force as they are the greater. And if the sky seems to us so feeble in comparison with what it is, it may be that the capacity which we have of perceiving is too feeble to have a lively and sensible perception of its entire size. For it is certain that the more lively our perceptions are the more they participate in our mind and the more they fill our capacity to perceive or to think---a capacity which certainly has very strict limits. The idea of the infinite in extension embraces, therefore, more reality than that of the sky; and the idea of the infinite in all genera of being, that which responds to the word Being, infinitely perfect Being, contains it still more infinitely, although the perception with which this idea affects us be the most feeble of all; as feeble as it is vast, and consequently, infinitely feeble, for it is infinite.

In order that you may better comprehend all of this, the reality and efficacy of ideas, it is well that you reflect many times upon two truths. The first, that one never sees objects in themselves, and that one does not even feel his own body in itself, but only through its idea. The second, that the same idea can affect us with entirely different perceptions.

The proof that one never sees objects in themselves is evident: for one often sees those which do not exist at all outside, as when one is sleeping, or when the brain is too inflamed by some illness. What one sees, then, is certainly not the object, since the object does not exist; and nothingness is not visible; for to see nothing and not to see is the same thing. It is therefore by the action of ideas on our mind that we see objects. It is also by the action of ideas that

71

we feel our own body.  For there are a thousand
experiences among people who have lost an arm
and who still feel long afterwards that their
hand hurts.  Certainly the hand which thus affects them and which affects them with a feeling
of pain is not the one which has been removed.
It can only be, therefore, the idea of the hand
in consequence of the disturbance of the brain,
similar to those which we have when we injure our
hand.  It is, in effect, that the matter of which
our body is composed cannot act on our mind. Only
he can who is superior to it and who has created
it, who draws it by the idea of the body, that
is, by his own essence insofar as it is representative of extension; which I shall explain to you
in time.

It is moreover certain that the same idea may
affect our soul with entirely different perceptions
For if your hand be in water that is too warm,
and if at the same time you should have the gout
in it, and further, if you look at it, the idea
of the same hand will affect you with three different feelings, pain, heat and color.  Hence,
one must not judge that the idea one has when one
thinks of extension with closed eyes, would be
different from that which one has when one opens
them in the middle of a field; it is only the
same idea of extension which affects us with different perceptions.  When your eyes are closed,
you have only a very feeble perception or a pure
intellection, and always of the same diverse
ideal parts of extension.  But when they are open,
you have diverse sensible perceptions which are
diverse colors, which lead you to judge of the
existence and the variety of bodies.  Because the
operation of God in you is not at all sensible,
you attribute to the objects which you do not
perceive at all in themselves the entire reality
which their ideas represent to you.  Now all this
is done in consequence of the general laws of the
union of soul and body.  But it would be too long
a digression to explain to you the details of all
this.

Returning to our subject, what I am saying may be even more clear if you reflect harder upon it. Do you still believe that to think of the infinite is to think of nothing, is to perceive nothing?

THE CHINESE. I am thoroughly convinced that when I think of the infinite I am far from thinking of nothing. But then I do not think of a kind of being, a particular and determined being. Now, the God which you adore, is it not a kind of being, a particular being?

THE CHRISTIAN. The God that we adore is not a kind of being in this sense, that his essence is limited. He is rather all being. But he is a kind of being in this sense, that he is the only being which embraces in the simplicity of his essence all there is of reality or perfection in all beings, which are only infinitely limited participations (I do not say parts), infinitely imperfect limitations, of his essence. For it is a property of infinite Being to be one and in a sense all things, that is, perfectly simple without any composition of parts, of realities, of perfections, and imitable or imperfectly participable in an infinity of ways by different beings.

No finite mind will be able to comprehend this clearly; but any mind, although finite, can clearly deduce this from the idea of the infinitely perfect Being. This is what you yourselves believe, that your Li, your sovereign wisdom, law, truth is a composite of several different realities, of all the different ideas that it reveals to you. For I have heard it said that the majority of your Doctors believe that it is in the Li that you see all that you see.

THE CHINESE. We find in the Li many things which we cannot comprehend, among others, the connection between its simplicity and its multiplicity. But we are certain that there is a wisdom and a sovereign law which enlightens us

73

and which rules everything. You apparently place
this wisdom in your God, while we believe that it
subsists in matter. Matter certainly exists. But
up till now we have not been at all convinced of
the existence of your God. It is true that the
proof that you give me of his existence is very
simple and such that I do not know at this moment
how to answer it. But it is so abstract that it
does not convince me at once. Do you not have one
that is more sensible?

THE CHRISTIAN. I will give you as many as you
please. For there is no visible thing in the
world that God has created from which one could
not elevate himself to a knowledge of the Creator,
provided one reasons rightly. And certainly I
shall convince you of his existence, provided that
you observe this condition---take note---to follow
me and not to reply to anything unless you conceive it distinctly.

When you open your eyes in the middle of a field,
in the very instant that you open them you discover a very large number of objects, each according to its size, its shape, its movement or its
rest, its nearness or distance; and you discover
all these objects by the perceptions of entirely
different colors. Let us inquire what is the
cause of such quick perceptions that we have of so
many objects. This cause cannot be but either
these very objects and the organs of our body
which receive their impressions, or our soul, if
you distinguish it at this moment from these organs, or the Li, or the God that we adore and whom
we believe to act unceasingly in us on the occasion
of the impressions of objects on our body.

1. I believe that you will agree that the objects themselves do nothing more than reflect the
light toward our eyes. 2. Since I suppose that
you know how the eyes are made, I believe that
you will agree further that they do nothing more
than collect the rays which are reflected from
each point on the objects in as many points on the

74

ptic nerve where the seat of the transparent
umors of the eye is found.  Now, it is evident
hat this reunion of the rays does no more than
isturb the fibers of this nerve and through it
he parts of the brain where these nerves end,
nd also the animal spirits, those tiny bodies
hich can exist within these fibers.  Now, thus
ar there is no feeling, nor any perception of
bjects.

THE CHINESE.  It is this that our Doctors deny
ou.  For what we call spirit or soul is, accord-
ng to them, only organized and refined matter.
he disturbances of the brain fibers together with
he movements of these small bodies, or animal
pirits, are the same thing as our perceptions,
ur judgments, and our reasonings.  In a word,
hey are the same thing as our diverse thoughts.

THE CHRISTIAN.  You stop me short; but you ne-
lect the prescribed condition.  You answer what
ou do not conceive of clearly; for I conceive
learly everything to the contrary.  I conceive
learly by the idea of extension or matter that
t is capable of figures and movements, of rela-
ions of distance, either permanent or successive,
nd nothing more; and I do say only what I clear-
y conceive.  I even find that there is less con-
ection between the movement of the small bodies,
he disturbances of the fibers of our brain, and
ur thoughts, than between the square and the
ircle which no man ever takes the one for the
ther.  For the square and the circle agree at
east in that both are modifications of the same
ubstance.  But the diverse disturbances of the
rain and of the animal spirits which are modi-
ications of matter agree in nothing with the
houghts of the mind, which are certainly modi-
ications of another substance.

I call that a substance which we can perceive
lone without thinking of something else, and
odifications of substance, or manner of being,
hat which we cannot perceive alone.  Thus, I say

that matter or created extension is a substance, because I can think of extension without thinking of anything else; and I say that figures, that roundness for example, is only a modification of substance; because we cannot think of roundness without thinking of extension, for roundness is nothing but the very extension so fashioned. Now, just as we can have joy, sadness, pleasure, pain without thinking of extension, so we can perceive, judge, reason, believe, hope, hate, and love without thinking of extension, I mean without perceiving extension, not in the objects of our perceptions, objects which can have extension, but in the very perception of these objects.

It is clear that our perceptions are not modifications of our brain, which is but diversely configured extension, but uniquely of our mind, the only substance capable of thought. It is true nevertheless that we nearly always think in consequence of what happens in our brain, whence one may conclude that our mind is united to it, but never that our mind and our brain are one and the same substance. In good faith, do you conceive that the diverse arrangements and movements of small or large bodies are diverse thoughts or diverse feelings? If you conceive it clearly, tell me in what arrangement of the brain fibers consists joy or sadness, or whatever other feeling you please?

THE CHINESE. I acknowledge that I do not conceive it at all clearly. But it is still necessary that it be so, and that our perceptions be only modifications of matter. For when a needle, for example, pricks our finger we feel pain and we feel it in the pricked finger; a certain mark that the pain is the sting and that the pain is only in the finger.

THE CHRISTIAN. I do not agree at all. Since the needle is pointed, I agree that it makes a hole in the finger; for I conceive that clearly, since one extension is impenetrable to every other

76

xtension. It is a contradiction that two are
nly one. Thus, it is not possible that two cubic
eet of extension can be only one. The needle
nich pricks the finger therefore necessarily
akes a hole in it. But that the hole in the
inger be the same thing as the pain that one
uffers, and that this pain be in the pricked
inger, or be a modification of the finger, I do
ot at all agree. For one must judge that two
nings are different when one has different ideas
f them, when one can think of one without think-
ng of the other. A hole in the finger is not,
nerefore, the same thing as the pain. And the
ain is not in the finger, or a modification of
ne finger. For experience teaches that the
inger hurts even those who have lost an arm, and
no no longer have fingers. It can only be, there-
ore, as I have already said, the idea of the fing-
r which modifies our soul by a feeling of pain,
nat is, this substance of man capable of feeling.
ow this happens in consequence of the general
aws of the union of soul and body which the Cre-
tor has established so that we will withdraw our
and and conserve the body which he has given us.
shall not explain myself further, for the con-
ition which I have imposed is that you must
nswer me only what you clearly conceive. I beg
ou to remember it.

THE CHINESE. Well, fine! Whether matter is or
s not capable of thinking, I would reply that
nat in us which is capable of thinking, our soul,
s the true cause of all these different percep-
ions that we have of objects when we open our
yes in the middle of a field. I would say to
ou that from the knowledge that the soul has of
ne diverse projections or images which objects
race on the optic nerve, it forms this variety
f perceptions and feelings. That seems to me
ery probable.

THE CHRISTIAN. It may seem probable, but cer-
ainly it is not true. For (1) it is not true
nat the soul knows that the object makes such

projections on the optic nerve. It does not even
know how the eye is made or whether it is con-
nected with the optic nerve. (2) Even supposing
that the soul knew all this, since it does not
know Optics and Geometry, it could not from the
projections of objects in the eyes conclude concerning them either their shape or their size;
their shape because the projections of a circle,
for example, are never a circle, except in a single case; their size, because it is not proportioned to that of the projections when they are
not at an equal distance. (3) Assuming that it
knew perfectly Optics and Geometry, it could not
in the same instant that it opens its eyes have
drawn this almost infinite number of consequences,
all necessary to place all these objects in their
proper distance, and to attribute to them their
proper shapes, without counting this astonishing
variety of colors that we see them covered with;
all that, today as well as yesterday, without
error or with the same errors and to agree in that
activity with a great number of other persons.
(4) We have an interior feeling that all our
perceptions of objects are in us without us, and
even in spite of us, when our eyes are open and we
survey them. I know, for example, that when the
sun touches the horizon it is not larger than when
it is at the meridian, and even that the projection
which is traced on my optic nerve is somewhat
smaller; and yet, despite my knowledge, I see them
much larger. I believe that it is at least a
million times larger than the earth, and I see it
smaller beyond comparison. If I walk from West
to East in looking at the moon, I see that it
advances in the same direction as I; and yet I
know that it goes to set to the West. I know that
the height of the image which is impressed on my
eye of a man who is ten feet from me diminishes
by half when he approaches to five feet; and yet
I see him always of the same size---and all that
independently of the knowledge of the reasons
upon which are based the perceptions which we have
of all  these objects. For many people who perceive
objects better than those who know optics do not

know these reasons. It is therefore evident that it is not the soul which gives to itself this variety of perceptions which it has of objects when it opens its eyes in the middle of a field.

THE CHINESE. I declare that it must then be the Li.

THE CHRISTIAN. Yes, without doubt, if by the Li you understand a being, infinitely powerful, intelligent, acting always in a uniform manner, in a word, infinitely perfect Being. Notice above all two things. First, that it is necessary that the cause of all perceptions we have of objects must know perfectly both Geometry and Optics, how the eyes and the members of the bodies of all men are composed, and the diverse changes which occur there at every moment, I mean at least those upon which it is necessary to base our perceptions. Second, that this cause reasons so rightly and quickly that one sees clearly that it is infinitely intelligent, a quality that you refuse to the Li, and that it reveals immediately the most remote consequences of principles according to which it acts unceasingly in all men and in an instant.

To enable you to conceive more distinctly what I think about it, I say that assuming that it is I who give the perception of distance of an object which is only three or four feet from me, it is necessary that I first know Geometry, how my eyes are composed, and the changes which occur in them, and that I reason thus. By means of the knowledge which I have of my eyes, I know the distance which is between them. I also know by their situation the two angles that their axis, which converge at the same point of the object, makes with the distance of my eyes. Behold therefore three things understood in a triangle, its base and two angles. Therefore, the perpendicular drawn from the point of the object over the center of the distance between my eyes, which marks the distance of the object which is directly opposed

to me, can be understood by the knowledge that I
have of Geometry. For this science informs me
that a triangle is determined when a side is given
with two angles and that from that one can deduce
what I seek concerning it. But if I close one
eye, since there are no more than two things under-
stood---the distance of the eyes and one angle---
the triangle would be indeterminate, and, consequently, I would no longer by this means perceive
the distance of the object. I could know it by
another, but less exactly, as by this latter. By
knowledge, granted that I know what happens in
my eyes, I know the size of the image which is
represented in the base of my eye. Now, Optics
informs me that the farther objects are the smaller are their images or projections. Therefore,
by the size of the image I must judge that the
object whose ordinary size I know approximately
in other respects, is also approximately at that
distance. But because this means is not very
exact, I must use both my eyes in order to know
more exactly the distance of the object. Likewise,
when a man approaches me, I judge by the preceding
means or similar ones that his distance from me
diminishes. But since by the knowledge I have of
what happens in my eyes I know that the projection
which is traced in the base of my eyes increases
in proportion as he is closer, and since Optics
informs me that the heights of images of objects
are in reciprocal proportion to their distances,
I judge rightly that I must give to myself a perception of this man that is always of equal size,
although his image diminishes unceasingly in my
optic nerve. When I regard an object and when
the projection which is traced in the base of my
eye changes place unceasingly, I must perceive
that this object is in motion. But if I walk
while I look at it, since I know also the quantity
of movement that I give myself, although the image
of this object changes place in the base of my
eyes, I must see it immobile; and if I know only
the movement that I give myself in walking, the
image of this object is not proportioned to the
change of place that I know occupies my optic

erve.

It is evident that if I do not know exactly
the size of the projections which are traced on
the optic nerve, the situation and the movement
of my body, and know divinely so to speak, Optics
and Geometry, when it should depend on me to form
within myself the perceptions of objects, I could
never perceive the distance, shape, situation and
movement of any body. Therefore, it necessarily
follows that the cause of all the perceptions
that I have when I open my eyes in the middle of
a field knows exactly all that, since all our
perceptions are regulated only by that cause.
Thus the invariable rule of our perceptions is a
perfect Geometry or Optics; and their occasional
or natural cause is uniquely what transpires in
our eyes and in the situation and movement of our
body. For if I were carried for example, by a
movement so uniform, as one sometimes is in a
boat, that I do not feel this movement, the shore
would seem to me to move. Likewise, if I look
at an object through a convex or concave glass
which enlarges or diminishes the image which is
traced in the eye, I would always see it either
larger or smaller than it is. And although I
know in other respects the size of this object, I
would never have a sensible perception save one
proportioned to the image which is formed in my
eyes. It is that the God whom we adore, the Creator of our souls and bodies, in order to unite
these two substances, of which man is composed,
has legislated a general law to give us at each
instant all the perceptions of sensible objects
which we would have to give to ourselves if we
knew perfectly Geometry and Optics, as well as all
that occurs in our eyes and in the rest of our
body. We can besides that, solely in consequence
of this knowledge, act on ourselves and there
produce all our sensations by relation to these
objects. In effect, God, having made us to occupy
ourselves with him and with our duties toward him,
has willed us to learn without application on our
part, by the short and certain way of sensations,

all that is necessary to us for the conservation
of life; not only the presence and situation of
objects which surround us, but even their diverse
qualities, whether useful or harmful.

Give now serious attention to the multitude of
sensations which we have of sensible objects, not
only by sight but by the other senses; to the
quickness with which they produce themselves in
us; to the exactitude with which they inform us,
to the diverse degrees of force or of liveliness
of these sensations, proportioned to our needs,
not only in you and in me, but in all men---and
that at each instant. Consider, finally, the
invariable rules and the general laws of all our
perceptions and admire profoundly the intelligence and the infinite power of God whom we adore,
the uniformity of his guidance, his goodness
toward men, his care for their needs in regard
to the present life. But note that his paternal
goodness, which our Religion teaches us he has
for his children, is above all this! A worker
no doubt loves infinitely more his child than
his work.

THE CHINESE. It seems to me that your doctrine
resembles closely that of our own sect, and that
the Li and the God that you honor have much in common. The people of this land are idolators. They
invoke the stone and the wood, or certain particular gods that they imagine to be in a position to
help them. I believe that his Lord of Heaven
also, whom you call your God is of the same kind,
more excellent and more powerful, but always an
imaginary God. But I see very well that your religion merits serious examination.

THE CHRISTIAN. Compare, therefore, without
bias your doctrine with ours. You are more especially obliged to do so since your eternal happiness depends on such an examination. The religion
that we follow is not a production of our mind.
It has been taught to us by this sovereign truth
which you call the Li, and it has confirmed it by

82

a great number of miracles, which you regard as fables, prejudiced as you are by the sublimity of your knowledge. I am trying to disabuse you by human reasonings. But do not believe that our faith depends on them. It is based on divine authority and proportioned to the capacity of all men.

You say that the Li is the sovereign truth. I too say this; but notice how I mean it. God, infinitely perfect being, contains in himself all there is of reality or of perfection, as I have already both proved and explained to you. He can affect me by his efficacious realities, for there is nothing impotent in God, that is, he can affect me by his essence, being that it is participable by all beings, by revealing to me or representing to me all beings. I say in affecting me, for although my mind be capable of thinking or of perceiving, it cannot perceive anything except what affects or modifies it. And such is its greatness that only its Creator can act immediately upon it. It is in the true Li that the life of intelligences is to be found, the light which illumines them. But this is what carnal and gross men do not comprehend. That is why I say that the true Li is the supreme truth. He embraces in his essence, being only imperfectly imitable in an infinity of ways, the ideas or the archtypes of all beings, and he reveals to us these ideas. Remove ideas and you remove truths, for it is evident that truths are only the relations between ideas. God is also the sovereign truth in this sense that he cannot deceive us, break his promises, etc. But it is not necessary to remain with these diverse senses according to which one may say that God is the supreme truth.

Tell me now, how do you understand the Li as the truth? But be attentive that this word, truth, signifies only a relation. For "two plus two are four" is truth only because there is a relation of equality between two and two and four. Similarly, "two plus two do not make five"

83

is also a truth only because there is a relation
of inequality between two and two and five. What,
therefore, do you understand by sovereign truth
or supreme relation? What kind of being is it?
What reality do you find in a relation, or a supreme relation? If one body is double another,
I conceive that it has more reality. But remove
the reality of bodies and you remove their relation. The relation between bodies is not fundamentally anything more than the bodies themselves.
Thus, the Li cannot be the sovereign truth, because being infinitely perfect, it embraces within
the simplicity of its essence the ideas of all the
things which it has created and can create.

You say that the Li cannot subsist except in
matter. Is it because you pretend that it consists only in the diverse figures which bodies
have and which compose the universe, and that the
Li is merely the order and arrangement among them?
What a small thing your Li would be if it con-
sisted only in that! And how much above this Li
about which you confess so many wonders, matter
itself, the least and most contemptible substance,
would be. For assuredly the substance is better
than these diverse arrangements, and that which
does not perish is better than that which is
perishable.

THE CHINESE. By the Li we understand not simply
the arrangement of matter, but this sovereign wisdom which arranges in a marvelous order the parts
of matter.

THE CHRISTIAN. In that respect your doctrine
is similar to ours. But why do you hold that the
Li does not subsist in itself and that it cannot
subsist except in matter, that it is not intelligent and that it knows neither what it is nor
what it does? That leads us to judge that you
believe that the Li is merely the shape and the
arrangement of bodies, for the shape and arrangement of bodies cannot subsist without the bodies
themselves and lack intelligence. The roundness,

84

for example, of a body is assuredly nothing more than the body itself so formed, and it does not know what it is. When you see a beautiful work you say that it has within it the good of the Li. If you mean by that that he who composed it was illuminated by the Li, by sovereign wisdom, then you think as we do. If you mean that the idea that the worker has of his work is in the Li and that it is this idea which enlightens the worker, then we would agree with you. But when one destroys the work, the idea which enlightens the worker always subsists. The Li does not, therefore, subsist in the arrangement of parts of which the work is composed, nor for the same reason in the arrangement of the parts of the brain of the worker. The Li is a common light to all men, and all these arrangements of matter are only particular modifications. These arrangements may perish or change, but the Li is eternal and immutable. It subsists, therefore, in itself, not only independently of matter, but independently of the most sublime intelligences which receive from it the excellence of their nature and the sublimity of their understanding. Why, then, do you disparage the Li, the sovereign wisdom, to the point of holding that it cannot subsist without matter? But even more, what strange paradoxes follow, if it be true that you hold this! Your Li is not intelligent. It is supreme wisdom, yet it does not know what it is or what it does. It illuminates all men, and it gives them wisdom and intelligence; yet it does not know itself. It arranges certainly the parts of matter for certain ends; it places in man eyes at the top of the head, so that he can see farther, but without knowing it or willing it. For it acts only by the blind impetuosity of its beneficent nature. This is what I have heard said that you think of your Li. Is it rendering justice to that from which you have all that you are?

THE CHINESE. We say that the Li is the supreme wisdom and the sovereign justice, but from respect for it we do not offer to say that it is wise or

that it is just. For it is wisdom and justice
which render things wise and just, and consequently, wisdom is better than the wise, justice
is better than the just. How, then, can you say
of your God, of the infinitely perfect being,
that he is wise? For the wisdom which renders
him wise would be more perfect than he, since he
would draw from it his own perfection.

THE CHRISTIAN. The infinitely perfect being
is wise. But he is in himself his own wisdom;
he is wisdom itself. He is not wise by an alien
or chimerical wisdom. He is to himself his own
light and the light which illuminates all intelligences. He is just and the essential and original justice. He is good and goodness itself.
He is all that he is necessarily and independently
of every other being, and all other beings have
from him all that they have of reality and perfection. For the infinitely perfect being is
self sufficient, and all that he has made has un-
ceasing need of him.

THE CHINESE. What, the supreme wisdom would be
itself wise! That seems clear to me to contradict
itself. For forms and qualities are different
from their subjects. A wise wisdom! How? It is
wisdom which renders wise, but it is not itself
wise.

THE CHRISTIAN. I see clearly that you imagine
that there are abstract forms and qualities which
are not forms and qualities of any object; also,
that there is an abstract wisdom, justice, and
goodness, which is not the wisdom of any being.
Your abstractions deceive you. Do you really think
that there is an abstract shape, a roundness, for
example, which renders a ball round and without
which a body, all of whose points on the surface
are equally distant from the center, would not be
round? When I render this justice to the Li and
say of it that it is independently of matter,
wise, just, all powerful, in a word, infinitely
perfect, and that I adore it in this quality, do
you think that in doing so I do not act justly

86

ndependently of your abstract and imaginary just-
ce, if in doing so I render to the Li the honor
hich is due to it? Once again your abstractions
eceive you. But I must explain to you how I con-
eive God to be his own wisdom and in what sense
e is our wisdom.

The God we adore is the infinitely perfect Be-
ng, as I have already explained to you, and
hose existence I have proved to you. Now, to
now oneself is a perfection. Therefore, the
nfinitely perfect Being knows himself perfectly.
onsequently, he also knows all the ways in which
is infinite essence can be imperfectly partici-
ated in or imitated by all particular and finite
eings, whether created or possible; that is, he
ees in his essence the ideas or archetypes of all
hese beings. Now, the infinitely perfect Being
s also all powerful, since omnipotence is a per-
ection. Therefore, he can will and consequently
reate beings. Thus, God sees in his infinite es-
ence the essence of all finite beings, I mean,
he idea or archetype of all these beings. He
ees also their existence and all their modes of
xisting by the knowledge he has of his own voli-
ions, since it is his volitions which give them
eing. Thus, the infinitely perfect Being is his
wn wisdom; he draws his knowledge only from him-
elf. And if he knows the matter which he arranges
ith so much art by relation to the ends that he
roposes, as appears evident in the construction
f animals and plants, he knows it because he
ade it. For if it were eternal, he would not
ave formed of it so many admirable works, since
e would not even have knowledge of it. The infinitely perfect Being can draw his knowledge
nly from himself. You see, therefore, how God
s wise and how he is also his own wisdom.

God is also our wisdom and the author of our
knowledge, because he alone acts immediately on
our minds and reveals to them the ideas which he
contains of the beings he has created and can
create; that is, because he affects our mind by

his ever efficacious substance, not according to all that it is, but only insofar as it is representative of what we see. To render more sensibly to you what I mean, imagine that the plane of this wall is immediately visible and by itself able to act on your mind and to make itself seen by it. I have proved to you that that is not true; for there is an infinite difference between the body that one sees immediately and directly, I mean, between the ideas of bodies---or intelligible bodies---and material bodies, those which one looks at in turning and fixing his eyes toward them. Supposing, I say, that the plane of this wall is able to act on your mind and capable of making itself seen by it, it is clear that it could make you see all sorts of curved and straight lines and all sorts of shapes without your examining the plane. For if the plane affects you only as such and such lines, and if the rest of this plane should not affect you at all, and should it become perfectly transparent, you would see the lines without seeing the plane, although you would not see the lines except on the plane and by the action of the plane on your mind, because in effect this plane embraces the reality of all sorts of lines without which it could not represent them within itself. Thus, God, the infinitely perfect Being, including eminently within himself all there is of reality or perfection in all beings, can represent them to us in affecting us by his essence, not understood absolutely, but taken insofar as it is relative to these beings, since his infinite essence includes all there is of veritable reality in all finite beings. Thus, God alone acts immediately on our souls; he alone is our life, our light, our wisdom. But he does not at present reveal them to us in himself but in the human sciences and in what is necessary in relation to society and to the conservation of our present life, sometimes in consequence of our attention and sometimes in consequenee of the general laws of the union of soul and body. He has reserved to us to teach concerning what has relation to the future life by his Word, which was made man, and who has taught the religion we profess. You see, therefore, that one does not deprecate the sumpreme wisdom, the true Li, in maintaining that he is wise; since he is himself wisdom and light and the sole light of our minds. But if the Li does not know himself and does not know what he does; if he does everything in the world by a blind and necessary impetuosity, however excellent his works may be, I do not see that in the dependence on matter in which you continue to place him that he merits the praises you give him.

THE CHINESE. I see clearly that it is not a contradiction that God is wise and also wisdom itself in the manner you have explained. But we conceive our Li further as immutable order, the eternal law, the order and justice itself. How can you still reconcile the Li with your God? How is he just and at the same time justice and order? Even our doctors do not know if your God exists; but the whole world surely knows that there is an eternal law, an immutable order, a supreme justice far above your God, if he is just, since he can be just only through that supreme justice. Our Li is a sovereign Law to which even your God is obliged to subject himself.

THE CHRISTIAN. Your abstractions still seduce you. What kind of being is this Law and order? How does it subsist in matter? Who is its legislator? You say it is eternal. You conceive, therefore, that the legislator is eternal. Further, you say that it is necessary and immutable. Therefore, admit also that the legislator is necessary and that he himself is free neither to form nor to follow or not to follow this law. You think that this law is immutable and eternal only because it is written, so to speak, in eternal characters in the immutable order of the attributes or perfections of the legislator, of eternal and necessary Being, of infinitely perfect Being. But do not say that he subsists in matter. I shall explain myself.

89

The infinitely perfect Being knows himself perfectly, and he loves himself invincibly and by the necessity of his nature. You cannot conceive the infinitely perfect Being otherwise. For his will is not, as it is in us, an impression which comes to him from elsewhere; it can only be the natural love that he bears for himself and for his divine perfections. It is for this reason that he esteems and necessarily loves more the beings which participate more in his perfections. He esteems, therefore, and loves man more, for example, than he loves the horse; the virtuous man who resembles him than the vicious man who disfigures the image of divinity he bears, for we know that God created man in his image and likeness. The eternal, immutable and necessary order which exists among the perfections which God embraces in his infinite essence, in which all beings participate unequally, is therefore the eternal, immutable and necessary law. Even God is obliged to follow it. But he remains independent, for he is obliged to obey it only because he can neither err nor deny himself, to be ashamed of the being that he is, to cease esteeming and loving all things in the proportion that they participate in his essence. Nothing obliges him to follow this law but the immutable and infinite excellence of his being, an excellence which he knows perfectly and loves invincibly. God is therefore just essentially, and is justice itself, and the invariable order (<u>regle</u>) of all minds which become corrupt if they cease to conform themselves to this order, that is, if they cease to esteem and to love all things in proportion as they are estimable and lovable, in proportion as they participate more in the divine perfections.

Since it is in the infinitely perfect Being---or, to speak as you do, in the <u>Li</u>---that we see all the truths, or relations, which exist between the eternal and immutable ideas that he embraces, it is clear that we see there the relations of perfections, as well as the simple relations of size; the relations which regulate the judgments

of the mind, and at the same time the movements
of the heart, as well as those which regulate only
the judgments of the mind; in a word, the relations which have the force of law, as well as
those which are purely speculative. Thus, the
eternal law is in God and is God himself, since
this law consists only in the eternal and immutable order of the divine perfections. And
this law is made known to all men by the natural union, although presently very enfeebled, that
they have with the supreme reason, or insofar as
they are reasonable. And more, by the feelings
of approbation or of interior reproach through
which this same reason consoles them when they
obey this law or grieves them when they do not
obey it, they are convinced that it is commanded
to them. But because men have become too carnal,
gross, slaves of their passions, in a word, incapable of entering into themselves in order to
consult attentively this supreme Law and to follow it constantly, they have every need of the
lights and succors of our holy religion. For not
only does she expose clearly all our duties, but
she also gives us all the aids necessary to ful-
fill them.

Compare, therefore, without bias your doctrine
regarding the Li with that which I have exposed
to you. Your Doctors were very clear, I agree;
but they were men like you and me. And we know
that there is a God, an infinitely perfect Being,
not only through an infinity of proofs that we
believe to be demonstrative, but because God himself has made himself known to the authors of our
scriptures. But laying aside for now the divine
authority of our sacred books, and that of your
Doctors, examine whether it is possible that your
Li without becoming ours, that is, the infinitely
perfect Being, could be the light, the wisdom,
the order which illuminates all men. Could we
see in him all that we see there if he does not
contain all reality eminently? Could one see in
a plane, if it were visible in itself, solids
which are not there at all? Is it not evident
that what one sees immediately and directly is

not nothing and that to see nothing and not to see
at all is the same thing? How do you find in your
Li these definite spaces, I mean, those which your
mind perceives immediately and which it knows to
have no limits, for I do not talk of these material spaces which one does not see in themselves
and consequently that one could see, or rather
believe that one sees, without their existing, and
to which you nevertheless attribute an eternal
existence which certainly agrees only with their
idea. For the idea of these spaces, or the spaces
which are the immediate and direct object of your
mind are necessary and eternal, since it is only
the essence of the infinitely perfect Being, insofar as it is representative of these places. You
say, therefore, as we do that the true Li which
immediately illuminates us, and in which we discover all the objects of our cognitions, is infinitely perfect and contains eminently in the
perfect simplicity of its essence all there is of
true reality in all finite beings.

You render justice to the true Li by affirming
in good faith that it is essentially just, since,
loving necessarily its essence, it loves also all
things in proportion as they are more perfect,
since they are more perfect only because they participate more in it. You say also that it is
justice itself, the Eternal Law, the invariable
rule, since this Eternal Law is but the immutable order of the perfections which it includes
in the infinity and simplicity of its essence: an
order which is the law of God himself and the rule
of his will and that of all created wills. But
beware of your abstractions, vain subtleties of
your Doctors. There are no such forms or abstract
qualities. All qualities are only modes of being
of some substance. If we love God above all
things and our neighbor as ourselves, in that we
shall do justly, without, if it may be said, being
informed by an abstract form of justice which subsists nowhere.

You believe that it is the Li who arranges mat-

ter in the beautiful order which we notice in the
universe, that it is he who gives to animals and
plants whatever is necessary for their conservation and the propagation of their species. It is
therefore clear that he acts in relation to certain ends. However, you maintain that he is not
wise and intelligent and that he does all that by
a blind impetuosity of his beneficent nature.
What proof have you of such a strange paradox?

THE CHINESE. This! It is that if the Li is
intelligent, as you think, being beneficent by
his nature, there would be neither monsters nor
any disorder in the universe. Why would the Li
allow an infant with two eyes to be born blind?
Why would he allow crops to grow only to have them
ravaged afterwards by storms? It is this that an
infinitely wise and intelligent being can change
at any moment by design, to do and likewise to undo what he has made. The universe is filled with
manifest contradictions, a certain indication
that the Li which governs it is neither wise nor
intelligent.

THE CHRISTIAN. Do you mean that he who has
given us eyes and has placed them at the top of
the head did not intend that we should use them
to see and to see farther? He who has given wings
to birds, did he not know or will that they should
fly through the air? Yet, you do not say, rather,
concerning the disorders in the universe, that because your mind is finite you do not know the diverse ends or diverse designs of the Li whose
wisdom is infinite. Because the universe is
filled with contradictory effects you conclude
from that that the Li is not wise. Yet, I conclude from it, demonstratively, quite the contrary. Here is why.

The Li, or rather, the infinitely perfect Being that I adore must always act in accordance
with what he is, in a manner conformed to his
attributes and which conveys his character. For
take care, there is none and there can be no other

law or other rule of his conduct than the immutable
order of his proper attributes. It is necessarily
in this order that he finds the motive or the rule
which determines him to act in one fashion rather
than in another; for he does not determine himself
except by his will, and his will is only the love
that he bears for himself and for his divine perfections. It is not an impression which comes to
him from without and which carries him without.
What I tell you is necessarily contained in the
idea of the infinitely perfect Being. Now, to form
for oneself general laws concerning the communication of motions, general laws of the union of
soul and body, and similar others, after having
foreseen all consequences conveys certainly the
character of an infinite wisdom and prescience.
And, on the contrary, to act at every moment by
means of particular volitions indicates a limited
wisdom and foresight, such as ours. Furthermore,
to act by general laws bears the character of a
general cause, uniformity of governance expresses
the immutability of the cause. That is evident
and resolves your difficulties. The Li, you say,
lays waste the crops that he made to grow; therefore, he is not wise. He makes and unmakes unceasingly; he contradicts himself; therefore, he
changes his mind, or rather, he acts by a blind
and natural impetuosity. You err. For on the
contrary, it is because the true Li always follows
the very simple laws of the communication of movements that storms form and ravage the crops, that
the rains, also produced by the same laws, have
made them grow. For all that happens naturally in
matter is only a following of these laws. It is
the same governance which produces such different
effects. It is because God does not change at all
his manner of acting that he always follows the
same laws, and that one observes in the universe
so many effects which contradict themselves. It
is by reason of the simplicity of these laws that
the fruits are laid waste; but the fecundity of
these same laws is such that they quickly repair
the evil that they have done. They are such, in
a word, these laws, that their simplicity and their

ecundity taken together, bear more the character
of the divine attributes than any other law more
fruitful but less simple, or more simple but less
fruitful.  For God does not honor himself only by
the excellence of his works, but also by the simplicity of his ways, by the wisdom and uniformity
of his governance.

God has established the general laws of the
union of soul and body in consequence of which,
according to the diverse impressions which are
made in the brain, we must be aware of the presence
of objects or of what happens to our body.  In the
brain of a man who has lost an arm there occurs
the same impression that he had while he had gout
in his little finger.  There occurs likewise in the
brain of a man who sleeps the same impression that
his recently dead father would have otherwise made
there.  How does it happen that this man is aware
of the presence of his father and that the other
still suffers the pains of gout in a finger he no
longer has?  It is that God does not will to com-
pound his ways nor trouble the uniformity and
generality of his conduct to remedy insignificant
inconveniences.

In consequence of the same laws, whenever a man
wills to move his arm it moves, without the man
knowing more than what he should do to move it.
One can see clearly that the end of this law is
necessary to the conservation of life and of
society.  But whence it happens that there is no
exception and that God, who commands charity and
forbids killing, concurs equally with him who
extends his hand to succor his neighbor and with
him who kills his enemy.  It is assuredly that
God does not will to alter his ways, their simplicity and their generality, and that he reserves
to the day of his vengeance to punish the crimin-
al abuse that men make of the power that he com-
municates to them by the establishment of these
laws.

Do not imagine that the world is the most excellent work that God could make, but that it is

the most excellent that God could make by means as simple and as wise as those of which he has availed himself. Compare, if you can, the work with the means, the entire work and in all times with all their means; for what God has chosen is the composite of the entire work joined to the means, which more greatly bears the character of the divine attributes. For he is not determined to that work save by his will, which follows his motive and his law; but his will is merely his love which he bears for himself, and his motive and his law are only the immutable and necessary order which exists among his divine perfections. Since the infinitely perfect Being is self-sufficient, he is free to do nothing. But he is not free to choose evil; I mean, to choose a design that would not be infinitely wise, and for that reason to forget that which he truly is.

Do not, therefore, humanize the divinity; never judge through yourself concerning the infinitely perfect Being. A man who builds a house and who a few days leter demolishes it, indicates most probably by this change in his conduct, his inconstancy, his repentance, his poverty of foresight, because he does not act save by particular and limited volitions or designs. But the universal cause acts and must act unceasingly by general volitions and follows exactly the wise laws he has prescribed after having foreseen and wanted positively and directly all the effects which render his work more perfect, for it is by reason of these good effects that he has established these laws, but, after having foreseen and only permitted evils, that is to say, indirectly willed that they should occur. For he does not will these evil effects directly at all. He wills them only because he wills directly to act according to what he is and to conserve in his governance the generality and uniformity which agree with him, so that it should be conformed to his attributes. It is not the case, however, that when the order of these same attributes demands or permits that he act by particular volitions, he does not make them, as has happened in the establishment of our holy religion, for we know that it has been confirmed by many miracles.

The general principle of all this is that causes act according to what they are. Thus, to know how they act, instead of consulting oneself, it is necessary to consult the idea one has of these causes. Your Emperor is of the same nature as you. However, you do not imagine that he must act as you yourselves would act on parallel occasions. For if he should be glorified more for his dignity than for his nature, he could conceive designs which you could never think about. Consult, therefore, the idea of the infinitely perfect Being if you would know something about its conduct.

But you do not see, moreover, that it is absolutely necessary for the conservation of the human species and the establishment of societies, that the true Li acts unceasingly in us in consequence of the general laws of the union of the soul and the body, of which the natural or occasional causes are the diverse changes which occur in the two substances of which men are composed. Assuming only that God does not give us always the same perceptions, while in our eyes or in our brain there are the same impressions, that alone would destroy all societies. A father would not recognize his child and a friend his friend. One would take a stone for a loaf of bread, and generally everything would be in a frightful confusion. Remove the generality of natural laws and everything collapses in a chaos in which one knows nothing. For the particular volitions of the true Li who governs the world are entirely unknown to us. One would perhaps believe, for example, that by tossing oneself from a window one could descend as certainly from his house as by the stairs, or that in confiding in God, whose nature is beneficent, one could walk upon the waters without sinking. Do not judge, therefore, that the true Li acts by a blind impetuosity by

97

reason of the evils which happen to you. He
leaves to your industry, enlightened by the knowledge of general laws, to you to avoid those evils
of the present life; and he informs us so that we
may apprehend what is necessary to avoid those of
the future life which are more certainly to be
believed. He is infinitely good. He is naturally beneficent. He even does to his creatures, I
do not fear to say it, all the good that he can
do to them, but by acting as he must, beware of
this condition, by acting according to the immutable order of his attributes; for God loves
infinitely more his wisdom than his works. The
happiness of man is not the end of God, I mean
his principal end, the last end. God is his own
end. His last end is his own glory; and when he
acts it is to act according to what he is, always
in a manner which bears the character of his attributes, for there is no other law or other rule
of his conduct.

THE CHINESE. I acknowledge with you that the
Li necessarily knows what he does, and even that
he wills it; and I am sufficiently satisfied by
the response that you have made to the objection
which I have made to you. But you nevertheless
assume that matter has been created from nothing,
which I do not believe to be true for two reasons.
The first is that there is a contradiction in saying that one can make something from nothing. The
second is that I can affirm of a thing what I know
to be contained in the idea I have of it. For example, I can be certain that a square can be divided into two equal and similar triangles, because I conceive it clearly; thus, I can be certain that extension is eternal because I conceive
it as eternal.

THE CHRISTIAN. To your first objection I answer
that it is true that God himself cannot make something in this sense, that nothingness is the base
or the subject of the work, or that the work is
formed or composed of nothing, for that would be
a manifest contradiction. The work would be and

not be at the same time, which alone involves a contradiction.  But that the infinitely perfect, and consequently all powerful, Being (for omnipotence is contained in the idea of infinitely perfect Being), wills and produces consequently beings whose ideas or models are contained in his own essence which he knows perfectly, there is in that no contradiction, for nothingness and being can succeed one another.  God sees in himself the idea of extension; he can therefore will to produce it.  If he so wills and, however, it is not produced, then he is not omnipotent nor, consequently, infinitely perfect.  Deny, therefore, the existence of an infinitely perfect Being or agree that he could have created matter, and also that he alone has created it, since he moves it and arranges it in the order that we admire. For being infinitely perfect, independent, deriving his knowledge only from himself, and even knowing from all eternity everything that he knows must happen, if he did not make matter, he would not only not know the changes which occur to it, but he would not even know if it exists.

THE CHINESE.  I acknowledge with you that I do not comprehend the least relation between the will of your God and the existence of a straw.

THE CHRISTIAN.  Very well, what do you wish to conclude from that, that the infinitely perfect Being can not create a straw?  You therefore deny that there is an infinitely perfect Being, or rather, you agree that there are many things that neither you nor I can comprehend.  But in good faith you do conceive clearly some relation between the action of your Li, whatever it might be, or between its will (if moreover you agree that it does nothing without knowing and willing to do it), and the movement of a straw.  For my part I acknowledge also my own ignorance.  I see no relation between a volition and the movement of a body.  The true Li has formed for me two eyes marvelously structured and proportioned to the action of light.  When I open them I have, in

99

spite of myself, diverse perceptions of diverse
objects, each of a certain size, color, figure
and the rest. Who does all this in me and in all
men? It is an infinitely intelligent and omnipotent being. He does it because he wills it.
But what is the relation between the will of the
sovereign Being and the least of his effects? I
do not see this relation clearly, but I conclude
to it from the idea I have of this being. I know
that the volitions of an omnipotent being must
necessarily be efficacious to the point of being
able to do everything which does not involve a
contradiction. When I shall see God as he is,
which my religion leads me to hope, I shall comprehend clearly in what the efficacy of his volitions consists. What I conceive, moreover, is
that there is a contradiction in saying that your
Li can move a straw by his proper efficacy if the
existence of this straw is not the effect of the
will of the true Li. For if God wills and consequently creates or conserves this straw in that
place, and he cannot create it unless he creates
it in some place, it would be where he wants it
and never elsewhere. It comes to this. Only he
whose always efficacious will gives existence to
bodies can move them or make them exist successively in different places.

THE CHINESE. That is very well. But what do
you answer to my second proof concerning the eternity of extension? Is it not demonstrative? Can
one not affirm what one conceives clearly? Now,
when we think of extension we conceive it as
eternal, necessary, infinite. Therefore, extension is not created. It is eternal, necessary,
infinite.

THE CHRISTIAN. Yes, without doubt extension,
what you perceive immediately and directly, intelligible extension is eternal, necessary, infinite. For it is the idea or the archetype of
created extension, which we perceive immediately.
And this idea is the eternal essence of God himself, being but relative to material extension,

or being but representative of the extension of
which this universe is composed.  This idea is
not created.  It is eternal.  But the extension
in question, that of which this idea is the model,
is created in time by the will of the Omnipotent.
You still confuse the ideas of bodies with the
bodies themselves.  From the existence of the
idea which one perceives of a magnificent palace can one conclude to the existence of this
palace?

This proposition is true: one can affirm of a
thing whatever one conceives clearly to be contained in the idea of this thing.  The reason is
that beings are necessarily conformed to the ideas
of him who has made them, and that one sees in the
essence of him who has created them the same ideas
according to which he has created them.  For if we
should see these ideas otherwise, if each of us
should see them, for example, in the modifications
of our own substance, then just as God has not
made the world according to my ideas, but according to his own, I could never affirm of any being
what I would see clearly to be contained in the
idea I would have of it.  But from the idea one
has of beings one cannot conclude to the actual
existence of these beings.  From the eternal,
necessary, infinite idea of extension one cannot
conclude from that that there is another necessary,
eternal, infinite extension.  One cannot even conclude that there are any bodies.  The infinitely
perfect Being sees in his own essence an infinity
of possible worlds of different kinds, of which
we have no idea, because we do not know all the
ways which his essence can be participated in or
imperfectly imitated. Can one conclude from this
that all the models of these worlds are executed?
It is therefore evident that from the necessary
existence of these ideas one cannot conclude to
the necessary existence of beings of which these
ideas are the models.  One can only discover among
the ideas of beings their properties, because
these beings have been made by him himself in whom
we see their ideas.

101

# INDEX

Alexander VII, 5
Allan, Charles W., 33, 39
André, Yves Marie, 3, 6, 33
Aquinas, St. Thomas, 55
Aristotelianism, 9ff
Arnauld, Antoine, 1, 7, 8, 17-23, 34, 35, 39, 58
Augustine, St., 51, 55, 57, 58
Augustinian theology, 1

Bayle, Pierre, ix
Being, Idea of, 16ff
Berkeley, George, ix, x
Bodde, Derk, 36
Boileau, 35
Bruce, J. Percy, 36, 39
Buddhism, 5, 23

Chan, Wing-tsit, 36, 39
Ch'i, 24
Chih, 27
Chu Hsi, 2, 23-27
Cicero, 56, 58
Clement IX, 5
Clement XI, 6
Collège de la Marche, 1, 7
Confucianism, 2, 4ff, 8
Confucius, 23
Cook, Daniel J., 34
Creation, 19ff, 30, 56-60 98ff
Cuvillier, Armand, 36

Delbos, Victor, 36, 39
Descartes, Rene, ix, x, 1, 9, 13-16, 28
Dominicans, 3, 4, 6

Dortous de Mairan, J. J., 1, 21ff
Dreyfus, Genette, ix
Duyvendak, J. J. L., 33, 39

Error, 9ff

Fouquet, J. F., 6
Fung, Yu-lan, 36, 39

Geometry, 79ff
Ginsberg, Morris, ix
God...
    nature of, 28, 48, 50, 65ff, 73, 87
    existence of, 28, 69, 74
    and evil, 29ff, 61, 93
    and ideas, 13ff, 15-23, 50ff, 65ff, 88ff, 90
    and the infinite, 28, 48, 66ff
Gouhier, Henri, ix, 31, 34, 35, 36, 39
Granet, M., 33, 39
Great Ultimate, 24ff
Gueroult, Martial, ix, 34, 40

Hobbes, Thomas, 58
Holy Office, The, 5, 6
Hume, David, x, 1

Ideas, 10
    innate ideas, 13
    nature of, 11ff, 17ff, 52ff, 66ff
    source of, 11ff, 54ff
    as modifications of the soul, 12ff